BACK TO THE
UPPER ROOM

BACK TO THE UPPER ROOM

CHARLES M. IRISH

THOMAS NELSON PUBLISHERS
Nashville

Published in Nashville, Tennessee, by Thomas Nelson, Inc., Publishers, and distributed in Canada by Word Communications, Ltd., Richmond, British Columbia, and in the United Kingdom by Word (UK), Ltd., Milton Keynes, England.

Unless otherwise noted Scripture quotations are from The Holy Bible: NEW INTERNATIONAL VERSION. Copyright © 1978 by the New York International Bible Society. Used by permission of Zondervan Bible Publishers.

Scripture quotations noted TLB are from *The Living Bible* (Wheaton, Illinois: Tyndale House Publishers, 1971) and are used by permission.

Scripture quotations noted NASB are from THE NEW AMERICAN STANDARD BIBLE, Copyright © 1960, 1962, 1963, 1968, 1971, 1972, 1973, 1975, 1977 by The Lockman Foundation and are used by permission.

Library of Congress Cataloging-in-Publication Data

Irish, Charles M.
    Back to the upper room / Charles M. Irish.
      p.   cm.
    Includes bibliographical references.
    ISBN 0-7852-8311-0 (pbk.)
    1. Church renewal—Episcopal Church. 2. Pentecostalism—Episcopal Church. 3. Pastoral theology—Episcopal Church.
4. Irish, Charles M. 5. Episcopal Church—Membership.
6. Episcopal Church—Doctrines. 7. Anglican Communion—United States—Doctrines. I. Title.
BX5933.I75 1993
283'.092—dc20
[B]
                             93–2550
                               CIP

Printed in the United States of America
2 3 4 5 6 7 — 98 97 96 95 94

Dedicated to:

God the Holy Spirit who continues the work of making the kingdom of God available to us.

My wife Jan who has encouraged me to believe that I could do it.

My son Kelly who has followed in my footsteps as a servant of the Lord.

My daughters Tara, Shannon, and Shuvawn, who always make me proud.

TABLE OF CONTENTS

Ministry before Gifts
Preparing the People to Do Ministry
Testimony Tells of the Spirit's Presence
Ministry Principles
All True Churches Are Charismatic
Spiritual Gifts Lead Us Toward God's Will
Spiritual Gifts Build the Body of Christ
Start Small Without Haste
God Gifts a Barren Woman

Mistake After Mistake
Reasons Why People Don't Want New Members
Applying Pressure for Groups to Evangelize
Some Groups Still Not Convinced
Principles of Fellowship
A Reasonable, Holy, and Living Sacrifice

Servant or Leader?
All Begin at the Foot of the Cross
The Wrong Way to Select Leaders
Leaders Are Submitted to Authority
God Chooses Some Before They Are Ready
Leaders Are Committed to the Mission of the Church
Those Called Must Be Empowered
Leadership Traps
Leaders Are to Be Discipled First, Educated Second
Dispensational Teaching Robs the Church of Gifts
Enfleshing the Church's Vision
Beginning the Discipleship Process

Demanding the Best
The Doorway to Renewal
A Definition of Renewal
Measuring the Success of Renewal
If You Are Born Again You Will Know It
Being a Disciple
Leaders Getting the Right Attitudes
The Return to Apostolic Life

Mainline Denominations Have Lost Their Way
Only God Can Fix the Broken Church
Jesus Is the Builder of the Church

ACKNOWLEDGMENTS

With Thanks To:

The scores of people who have read, edited and encouraged the various manuscripts that I have produced over the years. There are too many to thank by name.

Bob Slosser who applied the pressure to make me do it.

1

GREAT EXPECTATIONS

Marrying a Childhood Sweetheart

"I love you. Will you marry me?"

I had written and asked Jan to marry me when I was twelve. Her dad was a bridge engineer. She had moved away, and my heart had gone with her. I think she had replied that she would marry me, but the years passed and she had forgotten. I had only re-entered her life when I was twenty-one and on my way from Bluffton, Indiana, to boot camp. She was living in Cincinnati, Ohio. The Korean War had broken out, and I knew that sooner or later I would be draft-bait. There was always that stirring within me to be a man. The Marine Corps ads made the strongest pitch, and in October of 1950, I was on my way to Parris Island. I stopped to see Jan, asking her to write me.

"I love you. Will you marry me?"

This message was written on the backs of the envelopes carrying my letters to Jan. She had refused me when I first asked her after I joined the Marine Corps, and I don't blame her. Even though we were childhood sweethearts age nine through age eleven, I was not a compelling kind of guy. Later, I would consider myself a nerd. However, the Marine Corps did a lot to change a mama's boy into a man. It wasn't an easy transition, but the drill sergeant's fist in my face speeded things up. My attitude about myself was changed through the Marine Corps' methods. The advertisement was correct: "Be a man, be a Marine."

"I love you. Will you marry me?"

Jan told me later that she always wondered what the postman thought as he delivered my letters. But it didn't really matter. My persistence paid off, and she finally said yes. On the banks of the Wabash near Bluffton, during a Christmas leave, I gave her a ring and we began to look forward to living our lives together.

Becoming a Man

Back at Camp Lejeune, my buddy Lloyd Smalley and I heard that we could volunteer to go to Korea. Others in our recon outfit were being accepted, so we offered ourselves. We wanted to see some action to prove our manhood. Men perform strange rituals at times. Both Lloyd and I were accepted for Korea. This, however, gave Jan and me a problem. We wanted to get married right away, because married servicemen get allotment checks that Jan could save while I was overseas. Jan's father consented, and we were married on July 12, 1952, just two weeks before I went to California to prepare for shipping out.

Jan was an Episcopalian, so we were married in an Episcopal church. From that time on, I considered myself an Episcopalian too, although I confess I didn't know much about the church and its practices. As do most military people who go to war, I began to get religious. Jan's pastor gave me a prayer book and a cross with the inscription, "Christ died for thee." It was deeply meaningful to me.

I remember how my newfound religious nature expressed itself while I was at the staging area in Camp Pendleton. I had climbed one of the tall hills near the camp and found a cross lying on top. I carved into its arms "Christ died for thee," and then I erected it, digging out a hole and using stones. I didn't know the real meaning of "Christ died for thee," but this act helped me to feel religious.

On the ship to Korea, I got out my little prayer book and read the prayers for my devotional life. I also read them so that some of the guys could see that I was religious. After all, what good is it to be religious if no one knows you are? There was one truth that came through it all, however: I did want religion to mean something. I desperately wanted it to mean something, for it's strange to pray to a God one does not know.

A Rude Awakening to War

When I first arrived at a camp in Korea, there was little time to be religious. Military chaplains didn't impress me. The ones I met were real duds. It seemed as if they were more interested in being religious, with a flavor of personal piety, than in bringing God to the midst of the men. Not all chaplains were that way, I later learned, but all that I met were. As a result, I didn't spend much time learning about God. I still did not know Him.

Lloyd got right into a recon company, where I wanted to be, but I was sent to a shore party battalion which was operating as an engineer company. Our main work was building bridges, bunkers, and roads and clearing mine fields. The mine fields caused many men to think about God. On the day of my arrival, a truck rolled into camp bearing the body of a Marine who had been hit in the stomach with a Bouncing Betty land mine. He had made a mistake, and the entire company was called out to see what mistakes could do.

A Severe Loss Awakens Religious Feelings

Lloyd was at a nearby camp. He was already a sergeant and doing well. I was only a corporal, but I had hopes. One December evening, I went over to visit Lloyd.

"Hi, Lloyd, how're you doing?"

Lloyd was as happy to see me as I was him. He had helped me when I couldn't keep up physically in boot camp and in my first months with the recon company.

"Just great, Chuck," he responded. "Got to go out tonight." He was cleaning a "grease gun" (a hand-held machine gun), giving it an extra polish job. "We have an ambush patrol. Seems there are some gooks who are giving a lot of trouble to our outposts."

That was the last time I saw Lloyd, for he was fatally injured saving a wounded buddy that night. I learned of it about a week later. I felt a deep grief, and I became more religious than ever. I was proud when the Navy Cross was awarded to Lloyd for his valor. Lloyd's death was a benchmark in my life. I had never before lost anyone whom I had loved. I began to write to his mother, feeling that I had to do something to make up for his death. Then I began to have feelings that I should do something for other people too.

That feeling was still with me when I got the news that our replacement draft was arriving. We were sent to the staging area where we were prepared for a return to civilization. This included getting de-wormed and de-loused. It was at the staging area that I learned that less than nine hundred of our eighteen hundred group would be returning. The others were either killed or sent home with serious wounds. I thought that God had spared me for some reason yet to be revealed. The trip to California was filled with impatient anticipation. I wanted to be back with Jan, but wondered what it would be like.

Starting Over

Thirteen months after leaving home, I was back. It wasn't easy to start our marriage again, even though we had written very often during the time I was away. I brought the Marine Corps home with me. Jan called it my "Marine Corps look"; I heard others call it the "great stone face." It would be a long time before the "Marine Corps man" would be just a "man." In the process, I lost much of my religious nature. Now I found the Episcopal services somewhat boring. I still didn't know God.

It wasn't easy to get back into college since I had flunked out of two. But now I wanted to go—that would be the difference. I returned to Ohio, where I was born and raised, to search for a college that would accept me. I had already been rejected by several colleges before I visited Ohio Wesleyan University in Delaware, Ohio. To my surprise, the registrar accepted me on face value. I am sure that he was responding to a veteran who was determined to start over. So it was there that I began to search for what would be my life's work. My uncertainty caused me to change majors several times. I finally settled on a philosophy major since I couldn't decide on anything better. One thing I did know: the GI Bill did not begin to cover the costs. Jan began to work for the university, but was soon pregnant with Tara, our first child. She worked right up until the Friday before the Monday when Tara was born. I now had to get a job. I finally found one with a home-building company as a house salesman. I arranged all my classes for the morning so that I could work from noon until nine o'clock, seven days a week. I was good at selling, and I became a star performer for the company, selling 113 homes in the first year. The commissions, however, were small; I made just enough to keep me in school and feed my family. I enjoyed the job although I never considered sales as permanent work.

A Call to Ordination

I did enjoy the Episcopal church in the college town. It was there that I was confirmed as a member. I especially enjoyed the rector, Ralph Putney, and his wife, Mary. I was becoming more religious. I liked the relationship with Father Putney and the church; consequently, I decided

I would like to go to seminary. I met with the bishop, and he gave me his blessing. My employer, for whom I had worked while attending Ohio Wesleyan, wanting to assist me in going to seminary, purchased land for a housing subdivision near Bexley Hall Divinity School. The subdivision was conveniently located in Mt. Vernon, Ohio, just a few miles from Gambier where both Kenyon College and Bexley Hall were situated. The plan was for me to build and sell homes while I attended seminary, thus giving me an income. He built a house on the property, which Jan and I purchased on the GI Bill. However, I quickly ran into a stone wall. On my first day at seminary, I went in to see the dean. I told him I had a job and was living nearby. I felt rather proud of my breadwinning capabilities. The dean's response took the wind out of me.

"I'm sorry, but you will not be able to have a job and attend seminary."

"But how will I support my family? I have to work if I go to seminary."

"I'm sorry, but those are the rules."

"In that case, I quit! There is no way I can attend without money." I left. I just couldn't believe it! I went home angry.

I stayed and built and sold houses near the seminary. The project developed into quite a large subdivision. That was the beginning of a successful career of building and selling homes in Ohio and Pennsylvania. Ideas of going to seminary almost vanished as I spent night and day loving my work. After working with this company in Ohio and Pennsylvania, an opportunity came for me to go with a home building company in Mansfield, Ohio. Although I thoroughly enjoyed my work, I continued to have nagging feelings that I should go to seminary.

One More Chance

It all came to a head nine years from the time I first enrolled in seminary. As I was driving home one day, it was as if God spoke to me. Now I was convinced. When I arrived home I told Jan that she should start packing up because I was going to go to seminary. I was surprised at her answer: "It's about time!" When I visited the local Episcopal rector to explain what I intended to do, I was rebuffed. He didn't think that I should go, making it clear that there would be no support from the church. Instead of being deterred, I was more convinced that I was to attend seminary with or without his approval. Yet, I had a problem. Without a sponsoring church I could not enroll. I quickly solved the problem by transferring my membership back to my previous church in Salem, Ohio, where the rector was more than happy to sponsor me. He and I visited the bishop who said yes, and I was off again.

This time things were different. As we returned to Bexley Hall Divinity School, we had four small children, $1850 of small debts, a mortgage to pay on a home we could not sell, and we had no prospects of money. This time there was no job security. But since I believed that God called me there, I could not have been driven out. Despite the sense of call, however, I still did not know Him.

Instead of requiring me to serve under another pastor when I graduated from seminary, my bishop gave me a church to serve by myself. He believed that I was more mature, seasoned with business experience. So, at Trinity Episcopal Church in Bryan, Ohio, I put what I had learned in seminary to work. On the surface, it seemed to go well. The attendance and the money increased slightly. That's what our leaders looked for. Some even thought that I was doing an outstanding job. And I didn't rock the boat!

2

ALL HOPE WAS GONE

Frustration Surfaces with a Flood

I felt like a fool!

There I was bawling my eyes out in front of the whole group. An artesian well of tears spouted forth. As badly as I wanted to, I couldn't stop myself. Some of the group moved closer to console me. My mind was racing. "How did this happen to me?" I wondered. Alden, the sensitivity group trainer, had only asked me a simple question.

"Where would you like to be instead of here?"

That's when it all happened. I just came unglued.

"It's the people," I blurted out. "I am responsible for so many people."

I hadn't realized until then that being the pastor of a congregation was getting to me.

Before I went to seminary, I was a success in all that I undertook. I did well as a leader in the Marine Corps and while in Korea was promoted to sergeant. After my discharge, I enrolled in the university, working my way through by selling houses nine hours a day, seven days a week. It was there that I learned how to be successful in business. Following graduation with a degree in philosophy, I stayed in the housing business with great success. When I made the decision to enter Bexley Hall Divinity School in 1963, my employer kept my job open for the next three years. He was sure that I would come to my senses and return to the housing business.

Jan and I arrived in seminary with four children, looking forward to the time of learning to be a clergyman. Eagerly, I learned what I was supposed to learn from the professors. I was convinced that I would do well as a pastor. While in seminary, I began to search for a closer walk with God, but that was squelched when my faculty adviser warned me to get off of my personal religion kick. I always felt that there was more to know about God than what I experienced, but I didn't know who to ask.

Being in a small town is like being in a fish bowl; the same people watch you day by day. I went to the same drugstore for coffee and conversation; I went to the hospital daily and rubbed elbows with all sorts of people. Therein is the problem: if you do well or poorly, everyone knows it. Deep inside I believed that I was doing poorly; something was drastically wrong. The information, however, hadn't caught up with my conscious mind. It took a session of sensitivity training for the truth to begin working its way out into the open.

It took some time in that first session before I finally ran dry of tears. I got hold of myself and basked in the comfort that poured from the group. Although I felt fairly good as I left the sensitivity session, there was a gnawing at my insides. Something was wrong, I felt; very wrong. I wasn't going to let anyone close again; the lid was securely in place.

For a time, I immersed myself in sensitivity group work; I even became a trainer. I was searching for something that was meaningful, something that would bring me closer to God, for I still didn't know him. The sensitivity training worked for a time. It was like a drug, making me feel better about myself and my work as a pastor. But like all drugs, the effect wore off and I was left to face myself again. Something was definitely wrong.

A Career Crisis

Finally, it all began to come clear. I had a career problem. I was responsible for the spiritual health of the people, and I knew nothing about spiritual things. I should be bringing people closer to God, but I didn't know how. I did everything my seminary taught me, and it wasn't working. I didn't know where to go for help. None of the denominational leaders seemed to be spiritual people. They were more concerned with social action, with psychology and sociology. They didn't talk about God. How could I go to them?

As I stewed with my problem, two things became clearer. I had two expectations about my leadership that went unfulfilled. First, no one had been converted to Jesus Christ through my ministry. I saw them converted to the church, yes, but never to God. Second, I never saw anyone's life changed significantly by God. These were things that you were supposed to see when you were a leader of a church.

I began to worry that the people would discover the truth about me. They would learn that I was a phony—not a real pastor. How could I remain as the leader of a church when I couldn't lead anyone into a deeper relationship with God? I knew I was a failure, and I hated the thought. How long would it take the congregation to learn the same?

Out of the Frying Pan and into the Fire

Action was called for; I had to do something before they discovered the truth about me. I did what other clergy have done when they faced the same problem: I looked for another church. I went to the archdeacon of the diocese, explaining that I wanted a change. Of course, because of the increase in money and numbers, he thought I was doing a good job. So he helped me get a small mission church in Bath, Ohio, called St. Luke's.

I was so eager to escape my present problems that I didn't bother to find out about the recent history of the new church. I didn't know that the man before me was kicked out and that the congregation was divided. It only took a few weeks for me to discover that I was out of the frying pan and into the fire. There were more problems to deal with than ever, and my ability to bring God's things to bear upon them was nil. Now I really was in trouble!

Soon I gave up trying. Instead of preaching from some biblical text, I began to use Rod McKuen's poetry. Soon I was offering modern music in church. One of my favorites was "Downtown" by Petula Clark. I was through playing the church game. "If God can't change people's lives," I thought, "then there is no reason to act like He is able." Strangely enough, the people seemed to like the change.

Time to Bail Out

After much soul searching I went to my wife, Jan. I had to tell her the truth.

"I've had it with church. I think that I should go back to school and become a psychotherapist."

That's what a lot of disillusioned clergy do. They still want to help people, but they can't seem to do it within the church.

"I think that I would like to enroll in the Primal Scream Institute in California. I've read their stuff and it looks interesting. However, I can't enroll till next September."

It was only October, so there was a long wait. I couldn't tell the congregation that I was leaving, for they might kick me out like they had the man before me. I needed the salary.

When Jan heard that I wanted to leave the ministry, her response was immediate.

"It's about time," she said.

The few years as a clergy wife had been awful for her, too. Though she had been eager for me to go to seminary, she was equally as eager for me to quit pastoring.

The decision was made! Now all I had to do was wait for September to come.

3

METHODISTS TO THE RESCUE

God Reaches Out Through a Worried Daughter

"I sure didn't know what was going on at the meeting tonight 'cause everyone there was speaking in tongues but me. They said that I could, if I wanted to, but I couldn't."

My daughter, Tara, was very upset as she recounted the story of a Youth for Christ meeting she had just attended at her high school.

As far as Jan was concerned, this was the capstone. She had been concerned before about this group and its apparent fundamentalist leaning. "Who was in charge of the meeting tonight?" Jan asked.

"Some fellow by the name of Tim did the talking. He gave me this book and wrote his name in the front." Tara handed Jan *They Speak with Other Tongues* by John Sherrill. Later that night, Jan's concerns increased as she began to read the book.

"You ought to look into that group and find out what they are doing," Jan said to me. "I'm not sure that it's right."

"What group?"

"That high school group that Tara went to. They were doing some strange things tonight."

In my mind, interest for religious things had all but died. It didn't bother me that something strange was happening in that high school group. After all, there were all sorts of religious fanatics abounding in our territory.

"Maybe sometime."

I tried to pass it off as quickly as possible.

"No, I mean it," Jan persisted. "I'm concerned, and I think that you ought to do something about it."

"I would if I knew who it was," I replied, hoping that my ignorance would get me off the hook. But that turned out to be a mistake—or a blessing—depending on how it is viewed.

"Well, I know who is responsible for the meeting tonight!"

I was caught. Unthinkingly, I had committed myself. In a few moments Jan produced *The Akron Beacon Journal.* The name was there. It seemed there was a rock group, traveling around to various high schools in the area, called "The New Men." The musicians would play and then talk about their conversion and their subsequent move away from drugs. They were also Pentecostal! That was why all of the "babbling" was taking place at Tara's meeting. The people responsible for their visiting the high schools were a Methodist couple named Gig and Marilyn Korver. Reluctantly, I phoned them.

God Arranges a Divine Encounter

"I want to talk to you about what you are doing in the schools," I said sternly to the female voice that answered the phone. "My name is Father Irish, vicar of St. Luke's Episcopal Church." I was hoping that the tenor of my voice would frighten her or put her off, but her response was quick and cheery.

"Why, we'd be happy to meet with you. Just tell us when."

"How about Thursday evening at nine o'clock," I retorted, hoping that the hour would be too late for them.

"We'll be there on Thursday at nine o'clock. Just tell us how to get there."

The week before that Thursday was a tough week for me. Jan became ill with pneumonia and was confined to bed. I had to care for our four children, cook meals, and clean the house. Things also happened in the parish that took a lot of my time and kept me up all night a couple of times. I was fatigued and began finding it difficult to concentrate and keep my eyes open.

Nevertheless, I did my homework for the meeting to come. That is, I did what I was able to do. I found that there was very little information in my library about Pentecostals. What information there was indicated that they were an emotional people who babbled when they got all worked up. Moreover, I had heard about "Holy Rollers" as a youngster.

There was other information which described the Pentecostals as one of the fastest growing sects in the world. Some sources indicated that it would soon become the third largest body in Christendom. That was something, considering it began only about sixty years earlier. I did read a few pages of Sherrill's book, but not enough to know much. I was not prepared for what was about to happen.

I was tired on Thursday evening, and my thoughts of what might happen expanded by the hour. I envisioned a woman with no makeup, her hair in a bun, and her dress below the knees. She would have a tooth missing in front and a wild look in her eyes. I expected the husband, who was also coming, to be slightly built; I could almost see him wearing baggy pants, an out-of-style brown jacket and white socks. Surely, I thought, I would be able to use my superior intellect and training to straighten them out.

About nine o'clock, I was standing near the front door of the church when the couple arrived. I was taken aback. A beautiful young woman, attractively dressed, with a tall young man, handsome and assured, came up the steps. There was an aura about them which radiated something for which I had no words. Surely this could not be the couple. But it was. I asked them to come to my office, happy that at least we were meeting on my territory. I hoped the books on my shelves might alone overwhelm them.

In my office there were four chairs around a coffee table, and here we faced each other. The beginning was awkward. I'm not even sure how it all began. I was amazed by the joy in Marilyn's countenance, mystified by her enthusiasm to answer questions. During the conversation I learned even more astonishing things. They weren't uneducated Bible-thumpers. Gig was a Ph.D. research chemist for a large rubber company, and Marilyn was a physiotherapist at a local hospital.

"We would like to tell you what God is doing today," Marilyn offered with a smile. "He is pouring out his Holy Spirit upon people all over the world."

How does she know? I thought to myself. *Where does she get information from—from God?* By now my mind was racing. I was supposed to be the expert. I had been to seminary. I was in charge of a congregation. Now this laywoman comes into my office and purports to tell me what God is doing today!

As Marilyn continued, she spoke of things from the Bible.

"What is happening is just like at Pentecost."

I was a functional illiterate when it came to the Bible, so not much of what she said connected with me. I had never read the Bible through. I had barely passed the Bible content exam in seminary, doing so on the sixth try, and only because I had studied previous examinations. Bible wasn't stressed much at my seminary.

"You see, the baptism in the Holy Spirit empowered people to do things in God's name," she explained. "You remember how the apostles went about healing people and making converts. That power is being poured out today upon anyone who wants it."

I had gone into that session determined to do something about these crazy people; but as things progressed, my heart stirred. There was a certain credibility to what they were saying. And much more than that! Like the trainer at the sensitivity training session, they seemed to be able to see through my facade. They saw the truth. They saw someone seeking God. And tell me about God, they certainly did.

At a later date, I gave a testimony about this meeting. I described how I had prepared to do verbal combat with them, how I felt intellectually superior to fundamentalists, and how unnerved I had become because they weren't uneducated.

"But that isn't how I saw it," Marilyn told me later. "We saw you as one seeking God."

It was ironic. I had been seeking the presence of God for a long time. I had become discouraged and finally disillusioned because I could not see God actively revealing himself in the lives of men. I had determined that I had to leave the ministry and the priesthood. And now, as though God was concerned about me, He had sent this couple with a message from Him! Everything they told me clicked inside my soul. God went into every file drawer of my mind. He opened up my heartache and distress and began to replace it with hope. Nothing was really clear, however, just the idea that perhaps God still does things.

I didn't want to let Gig and Marilyn know that they were getting to me. I tried to maintain my aplomb so that I would not lose face. I remembered the time at sensitivity training when I had fallen apart in front of the whole group. That was not going to happen again!

A Power-Packed Prayer

"Could we pray with you?" Marilyn's hands opened up as she said this. In her radiance, my heart melted even more. I didn't know what I could do but say yes. This was the first time that anyone had ever asked me if she could pray with me. It had always been the other way around. People were always asking me to pray with them. I kept a little book of prayers handy, *Prayers New and Old,* for such occasions.

It was Marilyn who began to pray. Later, I learned why. Gig was only a two-week-old Christian. At first, the prayer bothered me. She spoke as though God was right there in the room. I even had the urge to look up once to see if He was there, but I controlled myself. I wasn't even sure what we were praying about. I guess my mind had raced from thought to thought so much that I lost track of the message. But it did not matter; I had submitted myself to them—Marilyn praying aloud and Gig silently. Whatever they were praying about, I was with them.

Not too long after Marilyn had begun praying, she started to speak in another language. I didn't know anything about speaking in tongues, so it only sounded as if she knew another language. But during that prayer she reached out her hand and put it on my shoulder. When she touched me, I felt a surge of warmth through my body, and I was suddenly relaxed from head to toe. I felt as if I had taken a warm bath. I didn't want to tell them what had happened; I was still determined to maintain control. Little did I realize that I had already lost control! Something had happened that was larger than I, and I didn't understand it. When the prayer was finished, I had trouble raising myself up from my slouched position.

I have learned since that when a soul is open to God, He will enter it. Mine was open. My attitude was not, but that didn't make any difference. After the Korvers had finished praying, they went home. Now I had a chance to be alone. I sat for awhile pondering what had happened. I wasn't sure what it was, but something definitely had happened; somehow I was different.

A Strange New Language Pours Forth

Then I went into the darkened church and knelt down at the altar rail. For some reason I felt the urge to talk to God, to surrender myself to Him. It had been so long since I really spoke to God. Now I wanted to speak to the God who had touched me just a few minutes before.

"Lord, I don't know what this is all about, but I sure wish you would give me a sign."

I began to pray, opening my life to God, surrendering myself to him. No sooner had I begun to pray than my mouth was filled with a strange language that I didn't understand. It just felt good to speak it.

Something happened inside, but now my intellect began to interfere. I was confused. My mind was saying one thing, my heart another. I was speaking in a new language, and I wasn't even emotionally worked up. I could even think while it was happening. It was as though I were an observer to something that was happening to me. My intellect wanted to deny anything good, so my confusion grew. I discovered that I could start and stop this language at will. When I would start, the words were there. When I stopped, they weren't there. This was no babbling! This was no uncontrolled emotion! I wondered how those articles I had read earlier could be so wrong? I wondered why our reference books were so negative to all of this?

In order to put my mind at ease, I phoned the Korvers and told them what had happened and asked them what it was all about. Marilyn, who had answered, said, "Praise the Lord!" That didn't help my mind, but it did help my heart. At least I knew that my experience was the same as they had discussed. I wasn't alone.

After talking to the Korvers I didn't pursue the experience anymore. Something inside told me that it was all right; I could go home, and more would be explained later. I didn't tell Jan what had happened to me. How could I? She was ill. She was upset by Tara's experience; what would she think if I told her I, too, spoke in tongues?

I found Sherrill's book and began to read it and look up the Bible references. My confusion began to wear off. Now the peace of God descended and I knew, for the first time, He was part of my life, not just in concept and hope, but in reality and power. For the first time, I knew Him! That evening I awoke in the middle of the night praising God.

God had broken through into my life. I had been hoping that the kingdom of God was more than talk. Paul's words were coming true for me: "For the kingdom of God is not a matter of talk, but of power" [1 Cor. 4:20]. When God was not in my life I languished. Now I had come alive.

4

"DO YOU KNOW JESUS?"

Everything That I Had Hoped For

How alive I had become!

I discovered in the morning when I awakened that my life and my ministry had been changed. Little did I know how much the church on Yellow Creek Road was going to change. The days to follow would be out of this world!

That first morning, for example, a young woman came to my office. She had been a lifelong church attender, and she had again come to the church seeking answers. Previously I had sent her to a psychiatrist under whom she had undergone both personal and group therapy. Now she was in my office, crying.

"It's just no good. Nothing I do seems to help. My life is worth nothing."

Without hesitation I found myself saying, "Do you know Jesus?"

"What did you say?"

"Do you know Jesus?"

As soon as I said that, she began to weep copiously. I wondered what had happened. Finally I said, "What's wrong?"

"That's it," she replied through her tears.

"What's it?" I queried, not realizing that God was at work through me.

"I've always wanted a relationship with God and never thought that I could have one. I have been so guilty all of my life."

A spiritual light came on inside me; I realized why she was so guilty, even though she was faithful in church things. She had said "The General Confession" week after week, and she had probably done her own personal confession too; but the reason that she still had guilt was because she did not know the One who could forgive her sin. God was still a concept to her, not a reality. Not knowing how to do it from any previous instruction or experience, I found the Holy Spirit prompting me to lead this woman to Jesus. I told her about my experience the day before, encouraging her to surrender her life to God and to receive all that was prepared for her. In a very short time she met Him, confessed her sin, and to my astonishment began to speak in tongues. She left my office radiant.

That incident was my first confirmation that God had done something significant in me. When I saw someone else have a similar experience, then I knew that I was not strange. Many such episodes not only confirmed my own experience but gave me the faith to believe that God wanted to touch others, too.

An amazing thing happened to me during this time: I began to develop a hunger to read the Scripture. I wanted to know more about God. Each paragraph was more exciting than the last. One thing for sure, I knew that God's word was true! When Scripture said it happened for the apostles, then I knew that it could happen for me. I didn't know much about the work of the Holy Spirit, but I was finding out.

The incident with the woman in my office merely "took the cork out of the bottle." Each new day found others confessing Jesus as Lord and being filled with the Spirit. Each of them spoke in tongues. Suddenly I began to get worried. It was a great ministry, but if it continued, everyone in the church would find out.

I knew that I would have to tell my congregation what had happened. It was too great not to tell. By this time, I had learned of two other priests in our diocese for whom the Lord had done the same thing. They were on fire for God! I had never before seen an Episcopal clergyman on fire for God. From them I learned the story of Dennis Bennett, a clergyman from Van Nuys, California, who was kicked out of his church for speaking in tongues. It was national news, being reported by *Time* magazine.

I wondered what would happen if I told the congregation about my experience. I wondered if the members would get rid of me as they had the pastor before me.

Jan's illness was difficult for her to overcome. And though many radical things had happened as a result of the Korvers' visit, I kept the information from her. I'm not sure what I thought she would do. Later, I learned that the responses of others' spouses ranged from immediate acceptance to wanting to have the person committed to a mental hospital. Perhaps people are not always ready for God's kingdom to come too near.

I wasn't used to having God for a leader. It was new and scary. Before, He had been either a partner or a sub-partner. Now I knew He had the answer for all of life. There was nothing else I could do but obey Him. This was such a radical change for someone who always did everything his own way, who tried to be a self-made person.

Time to Tell the Congregation

There was only one thing left for me to do. I had to tell my congregation. And on one of the next Sundays I did exactly that. I recounted how Tara had come home upset, how Jan had prevailed on me to do something, how the Korvers had come and told me the things that they had experienced. But I became a coward and ended the story there. To my surprise the people did not throw stones. Many hearts were touched and excited. That day was January 8, only twenty-two days after my own experience. Jan was still ill and did not attend on that day. I was relieved that no parish gossip reached her.

After that Sunday, the Lord really began to work on my heart. He kept telling me that I must tell all. Two Sundays later, I told the whole story. I told my congregation about my speaking in tongues and how it had changed not only my life but also my ministry. Jan was there to hear it for the first time. In the middle of the talk, I looked up and saw my immediate boss, the archdeacon of the Diocese of Ohio. I thought, *Well, here I go now.*

Seeing the archdeacon brought Dennis Bennett to mind. Would he kick me out? I was in a mission church. And the archdeacon was responsible for mission clergy. All he had to do was go back and tell the bishop what he had heard, and that would be that. I would be looking for a job. Later, the archdeacon came home to lunch with us. As we were entering the door I asked him, "Well, what did you think?"

Thoughtfully he replied, "We'll wait and see," and on that note I knew that for a time, at least, I was safe.

Jan, as I said, heard about my new experiences for the first time that day. But I think that she had already been affected by John Sherrill's book. She was not upset with me as she had been with Tara's situation. Although she had always been a traditional Episcopalian, she did not seem threatened.

Others Surrender to God and Are Filled with the Holy Spirit

On that Sunday I told the congregation that any of them could attend an interest group about the Holy Spirit the next evening. I planned to have the Korvers there and John Beckett, an Episcopal layman from Elyria, Ohio, I had heard about. I was surprised by the response. About forty-five people came to find out more about the Holy Spirit. Never had so many people turned out for a teaching before! I didn't know what to expect.

When John Beckett talked I got worried. He said things that I had never heard. He discussed such things as "the end times." He also talked about healing and the fullness of the Spirit. The Korvers also talked. I still had seen no formal ministry for the baptism in the Holy Spirit. Up to that moment it had always been a spontaneous outpouring when I prayed with people. At the close of the testimonies, Beckett prompted me, "Ask if anyone wants to pray."

I could tell that some people were really turned on and others were really turned off by the testimonies. When John asked me to ask people to pray I said, "Anyone who wants to stay and pray in the church may do so; those who have other commitments and need to leave may do so now." This was a wise move, for it let those off the hook who needed to escape.

About half of the people went into the sanctuary to pray. The rest went home. I was the last to come into the room, and when I did, I could sense an air of expectancy. I didn't know what it meant or what would happen, but I knew that something wonderful was about to transpire. People were quiet. I went in and knelt, not knowing what to do next.

"Why don't you ask if anyone wants to pray for the Holy Spirit?"

Beckett startled me as he whispered into my ear. I jumped up in my pew.

"Anyone who wishes to pray for the Holy Spirit should go to the altar rail." About twelve people moved to the altar rail as though they were being drawn there by invisible cords they could not resist. To my delight, Jan was one of the twelve.

Beckett led the people in a prayer during which they confessed their sin, and their willingness to follow Jesus Christ as Lord, and then they accepted Jesus into their hearts. I remember that they also renounced Satan and all involvement with the occult. The prayer ended with the people asking Jesus to baptize them in the Holy Spirit, since Jesus Himself is the baptizer.

I had wandered up to the rail so that I could see what was happening. No sooner had the people prayed and asked Jesus to baptize them in the Holy Spirit than the whole room seemed to erupt. People began to speak in other languages. One woman began to sing in a glorious voice. Pentecost had arrived at St. Luke's! I knew it, but I had apprehension about how the Lord's will could be done through it all.

As Blanche began to sing in a new language, Teresa, who was next to me, began to shiver and get restless.

"What's wrong?" I asked, looking at her.

"I can't tell you," she replied, not looking at me. I could clearly see that she was distressed. Right in the middle of the glorious outpouring of the Holy Spirit, she was distressed—beside herself.

"Look, I know something is wrong. What is it?"

"I can't tell you."

Throughout the evening I tried to get her to tell me the problem, but she refused.

It was almost a week later that I learned what was bothering Teresa. When Blanche had sung out in tongues, Teresa understood what she was singing. Blanche was singing in Italian (Blanche doesn't know Italian), and Teresa thought that because she understood somehow the devil had gotten her.

"What did she say?" I asked with considerable interest.

"She was singing praises to God in Italian."

The devil seems to wait around for the miracles of God, ready to rob people of their blessings if he can. He had bothered Teresa, and now he was bothering Jan. She hadn't spoken in tongues that night, even though she had prayed; she became convinced that something was wrong with her or that God didn't love her. This became a struggle. For almost a month the battle continued. Every night we would pray for Jan's prayer language, and every night we had nothing but tears. I was frustrated; Jan was despondent.

Much of the problem came from the fact that we knew little about the ministry of the baptism in the Holy Spirit and speaking in tongues. We proceeded on the assumption that God would make Jan do it. We didn't realize then that people do the talking and the Holy Spirit provides the language. He doesn't force people. Rather it is as the 120 experienced at Pentecost when the "Spirit gave them utterance." Some of the translations speak of "ecstatic utterance," but this is not what it is. People do not go into a holy trance and speak in tongues while they are out of control.

Jan's Spiritual Language Breaks Through

Finally, the victory came. One evening, Jan was in tears because nothing was happening. She wanted to stop praying, but I insisted that we pray until something happened. Suddenly, as if a dam had burst, a language began to pour from her mouth. It came out very fast, sounding much like Chinese. Both of us found this to be hilarious, and rolled laughingly into bed.

I believe the Lord wanted us to have this struggle. It caused us to make every attempt to minister to people so that problems like Jan's wouldn't happen. We were more tolerant and patient when people did have problems. We learned to rely on the Lord. The last was the hardest for me, because I had always been so self-sufficient.

5

SPREADING THE GOOD NEWS

Getting Good Advice

I have thanked the Lord many times that there were others around who could talk with me about my new experiences with God. For there were some clergy from our diocese who, upon hearing that something strange was happening, began to treat me as if I were a leper. How could anything so good be that bad, I wondered, when one of my former friends made an unkind remark? I could not conceive why an experience with God made people so angry.

One of the first persons whom I talked to was the Reverend George Stockhowe, then rector of St. Martin's Church in Monroeville, Pennsylvania. He had a level head about things and encouraged me to persist slowly. One great piece of advice was to remember to have someone else do the hard work with the congregation, such as evangelism and the baptism in the Spirit.

"In that way," he said, "even if they get angry at the person who ministered with them, you still will be able to talk to them. But if you are the one who disturbs them, then you have lost your contact and will no longer be their pastor."

I needed a lot of encouragement at this time. Things were new to me. I wanted to do what God wanted, and I found it difficult to understand what that was. There were now those who warned me of the problems I was about to face. I knew everyone meant well, but I didn't think they understood what was really happening in my life. I tried to listen to them as much as possible.

Hostility to the Work of the Holy Spirit

One day I came home from the church to find a priest from a nearby city waiting for me. I could tell from the look on Jan's face that John had been somewhat unkind in his remarks.

"I've been hearing some strange things about you." John got right to the point. He had been a sensitivity trainer, too, and wasted no time boring in with his concern.

"I'm not sure that what you have heard is accurate, but I can tell you that God has done a wonderful thing in my life. As a result, my ministry has totally changed. John, you wouldn't believe the things that have happened."

"You have to watch out for those fundamentalists." John seemed to continue without noticing what I had said. He used *fundamentalists* as a derogatory catch word to dismiss the value of someone's religious experience. What had happened was so far removed from his concept of fundamentalism that I didn't even feel the need to defend myself.

"Look, John, when this couple came into my office a few weeks ago, I was at the bottom of a pit. I was ready to leave the ministry, to leave the priesthood, and to leave the church, for that matter. When they told me what God was doing, my heart melted, and when they prayed with me, God poured His Holy Spirit into me. Before I knew it I was speaking in another language."

I could tell that John was not going to be persuaded by such a testimony.

"John, I am so sure that God is pouring His Holy Spirit upon all who are willing to receive it that I know He will baptize you in the Holy Spirit if you merely ask Him to do it. If you are willing, I will prove what I say, for I have confidence in God." That was the first time I was aware I had such confidence.

I was amazed as John got up and followed me to the church. Since there was someone in the church at the time, we went into my office.

"Let's kneel and pray," I said.

Both of us got on our knees. Then I began to pray. I asked God to do for John what He had done for me. I asked Him to overcome any doubts my brother might have. I then led John in a confession of Jesus as Lord and Savior.

"Now, just ask Jesus to baptize you in the Holy Spirit, for He is the baptizer, not I."

"Jesus, baptize me in the Holy Spirit." As soon as John said that he began to speak in tongues. He was amazed and subdued. I was blessed to see how faithful God was. John and I then embraced.

I wish I could report that the kingdom of God came nigh unto John and he welcomed the encounter. Instead, despite the outpouring of God in his life, he rejected the whole experience, becoming more entrenched in his opposition to the work of the Holy Spirit. I could understand a possible motive for this, since sensitivity training depends upon the skills of the trainer. The human person is in charge. When God's kingdom arrives, God must be in charge.

There were others who warned me in some way about the dangers of what I was doing. Except for a few visionaries, most of the reactions to the outpouring of the Holy Spirit were doubt, caution, concern, and sometimes outright hostility. Some even went as far as to accuse those involved with the Holy Spirit renewal of being possessed of the devil. I know that the warnings of some people came from the best of motives. They included fears that people would be caught up in "emotionalism," that this binge into "fundamentalism" would split the congregation, because it was "divisive," that people would be drawn away from the "Episcopal faith," that this spiritual navel-gazing would prevent them from dealing with the more important social issues facing our communities and our nation. There were others who feared that this "fundamentalist" turn would deny our historical leaning toward sound intellectualism. But we were far from being fundamentalist. In my mind a fundamentalist could be characterized as "brainless Bible." But the liberals were just as bad, for they represented "Bible-less brain." I saw that what we were doing was much more balanced and could be characterized as "bibled brain." Others feared that some people might even become emotionally disturbed. Most of the critics agreed that this was merely a movement of man and like other such movements was doomed to die eventually.

Evangelizing with Boldness

I took George Stockhowe's advice and invited him to do a teaching mission on the Holy Spirit for three days beginning March 21. In the meantime, the Reverend Bill Worman, from St. Andrew's Church in Mentor, Ohio, called a meeting of those involved in "charismatic" renewal. Both George Stockhowe and John Beckett attended the meeting.

How I needed that meeting! Enough had happened, and I needed to talk with others who were doing the same things. We talked about our experiences. Each account was like writing a new chapter in the book of Acts. God was so wonderful. It was the first time that I had ever experienced times of real prayer with clergy. The anxiety began to lift concerning my future with God. Jesus was Lord of my life! There was no turning back.

Later, when Stockhowe arrived to do the teaching mission, the Lord had already done his work. The church was full, and the people responded well to the singing of the gospel hymns. I had a song sheet for the service that I had gotten somewhere, but I didn't know the songs. I had to ask Gig Korver, who was there, if he would lead the singing, which he did.

I had never heard someone teach for an hour at a time as George did, but I liked every minute of it. Most Episcopal clergy preach only twenty minutes or less. One part of the teaching that really impressed me was the discussion about those who tried to take away everything that was supernatural in the Bible. George said he once knew someone who cut out everything in a Bible that referred to the supernatural. In the end he had nothing but a Bible full of holes.

As George talked, I kept watching faces, wondering what people were thinking. At the end of his teaching, George told people that if they were interested in what he was talking about, they could stay on and there would be additional teaching with ministry following. A large group of people were moved to stay, and George taught for another half hour before he prayed with them.

I was amazed to see so many people come forward to the altar rail for prayer. Soon people were confessing Jesus as Savior and Lord, and then they were being baptized in the Holy Spirit. There was an excitement and a joy that filled the church such as I had never witnessed before. God had moved into our lives in a supernatural way.

Our Lord continued to awe us with his power, and many people were touched by him in beautiful ways. I never knew what to expect, for it was all in God's control. One evening, a large group of people prayed simultaneously for the baptism in the Holy Spirit. All at once, people began speaking in tongues. One woman began to weep, another began to laugh, a man became exuberant and spoke out loudly as he felt the Lord's touch.

Each of the three nights of the mission saw people coming and giving their lives to our Lord Jesus. Many were baptized in the Holy Spirit and spoke in tongues. The word had spread like wildfire as those who were touched brought family and friends to see what was happening. It was similar to the biblical event with Andrew, when the first thing he did after his encounter with the Lord was to bring his brother, Simon, to see Jesus.

Before the mission I had trouble believing that it would all work out. This was a new experience for me. Never before had I known an evangelist, and here I had brought one, George Stockhowe, to St. Luke's! I had anxious moments wondering about how I would be able to pay for it. But I shouldn't have worried. God knew our need and through our offerings we more than covered our expenses.

The following week Bill Worman had a teaching mission at his church, St. Andrew's in Mentor, with Dennis Bennett as the teacher. Bennett's appeal was more than I would have expected. Hundreds came and heard the message of the movement of God's Holy Spirit throughout the world. Dennis had a free day on Thursday, and this man of God came to preach at St. Luke's. It was as if the Lord had planned Bennett's coming for St. Luke's.

We did not have time to advertise. But word of mouth did its work, and again our church was filled. Among the many who came forward during an altar call to receive Jesus and baptism in the Holy Spirit, fifteen were from St. Luke's. And my daughter, Tara, was one of them! Now, with so many having the same experience as I had, I got bold enough to call them together.

The Men Lag Behind Spiritually

On Friday, April 2, we held our first prayer and praise meeting. Thirty-five people were present, and we were now on our way to learning new things about God. The only problem about that first meeting was that only the women came. Jan and I began to pray, "O Lord, send us at least one man."

Women seem to have an eager responsiveness to things of the Spirit. They get way ahead of men. The trouble is that a strong spiritual woman is able to intimidate a spiritually weak husband. She is usually active in telling her husband what he ought to do, or how he falls short as a Christian, or how bad his sin is. All of it may be true, but truth shared at the wrong time only serves to turn away those who might otherwise be led to the Lord. In a simple way, the man is made to believe that serving God means to please the wife's desires, not God's. Instinctively the man knows this is wrong.

Our prayer was answered, but not in the way I was expecting or hoping. I was hoping for someone who was all-male, macho, who could win all of our men. Instead, God sent Dave Skeggs, an artist, who was not macho, and who I felt probably would not appeal to the men as I had hoped. Dave, however, was just what God ordered. He was just right for us and our needs. During the three years he was with us before he died, he demonstrated a zeal that still affects many today.

Slowly but surely, the women in the prayer meeting began to go home and love their husbands instead of judging them. The effect was powerful. One husband after another came to know Jesus as Savior and gave their lives over to Him as Lord. Many of them became leaders in the church. There is nothing more powerful than a loving wife, I learned.

Whenever we are faultfinders and straighteners of the bent and curved, we begin to take over God's work. He knows who is sinning and not serving Him; He doesn't need any help. The question is not "What am I doing for God in my marriage?" but "What is God doing with me in my marriage?" If God has hold of me, then I will be a blessing to my partner; if not, then I will be a curse.

I have since seen many marriage partners fail in this area with their spouses. They did not seem to make sense out of James' injunction that "the tongue also is a fire, a world of evil among the parts of the body." We make the mistake of placing our tongue in gear before our brain is engaged in hearing from the Holy Spirit. We begin to drive before we learn how to handle such a magnificent new gift. The rescue wagon has to be called out to take care of the casualties of those who have "foot-in-the-mouth" disease.

Learning about God on the Job

It is a thrill to take responsibility for the spiritual lives of so many people when one is new in the Spirit himself. There is so much to learn. How, for instance, can one lead people wisely and not quench the Spirit? What is praise? What is healing all about? What is prophecy? What should you do if someone speaks in tongues? How do you lead music? How can you find other leaders? There were so many questions, but the answers did not lie in the principles of spiritual leadership, which every leader needs to know, but in the Principal who creates principles. Unless Jesus has hold of the leader through the Holy Spirit, principles are without the Principal and, therefore, useless.

Of all the lessons I learned, the most important one is that Jesus is Lord. For unless He builds what is to be built in the church, He will have to tear it down. It is in relationship with Jesus that all leadership problems are solved, not in the amassed principles that I have written down.

Hundreds Come to Know Jesus

During the first years of our prayer and praise meetings, hundreds came to know Jesus as Savior, and they committed their lives to Him as Lord. They were filled with the Spirit and turned on to God. Most of them wanted to come to St. Luke's, for that is where they discovered Christ, but we kept insisting that they stay where they were, even if they were in dry places. This was a mistake because many of those people perished in the dryness.

I remember one teaching that I aimed at these people. It was titled, "How to Survive in a Dry Hole." But it was because of my experiences with frustrated people that I began to soften my stance somewhat on changing churches. What I taught was that you should always stay where you are, no matter how spiritually dry it is, when you believe that God has called you there. If you had no sense of calling, then you needed to go where God was leading. This is one of the reasons we told newcomers, "We don't want you at St. Luke's unless you believe God is calling you to be part of our fellowship."

Bob and Shirley were a couple who believed they were called to join our congregation. But it was not an easy decision. They were part of a nearby Episcopal church that never could get its spiritual act together. Bob, as its Senior Warden, was the chief layperson. First, Shirley was converted, then Bob. They were really excited by their relationship with God and knew that others in their church needed the same experience, for that's what Christianity was all about—relationship with God. They tried and tried to make a difference but were continually turned off. I encouraged them to stay and work it out, but finally it was necessary to assess where God wanted them to be. Their joining our congregation turned out to be a real blessing.

Later, I changed my thinking again on this matter. What I said was that if you could not be involved in ministry in your congregation, then you needed to make a change, for a person who fails to work with God will soon dry up.

6

LEARNING TO LEAD PEOPLE TO JESUS

Learning Evangelism by Doing It

People from all over the area began seeking out St. Luke's Church. The services were crowded, and the prayer and praise meetings were almost a standing-room-only affair. Individuals, young and old, were hungering for a vital experience with the living God. Slowly I began to learn how to lead people to Jesus. In seminary I was not taught how to evangelize people, so I had to go to the Pentecostals to get some practical education. It wasn't long before I got the idea, and soon I was very bold. What follows is a scene that was repeated time after time. How well I remember the joy of Mary's encounter with her Lord:

"What is Jesus saying to your heart now?"

"He's telling me that I must give my life to Him."

"Are you ready to do that?"

"Yes," Mary was crying.

"Now you know that God is here by the power of His Holy Spirit. He has touched you, revealing Jesus. See how much Father God loves you." With that, the sobs came in waves.

"I . . . I've never known love like this before. I can't believe that it's real." An honest statement, for how could she know what real love was—she had never experienced it before. Yet love was pulling at her heart—it was real. Not only that, it was personal.

The more the people came, the more I learned about evangelism and the bolder I got. This was the most important work that I would ever do in my life, so I wanted to be as good at it as I could. How I wished that my seminary had considered leading people to Christ important, too. How to lead a person to Christ should be a basic course. We will not move forward to make disciples of all nations until both the clergy and the laypeople learn how to do it. Clergy should be teachers in this matter.

The Kingdom of God Is No Private Matter

One of the first things that I learned went against all that I thought I understood. I came from a background that said religion is a private matter. Now I was learning that the kingdom of God is no private matter. I said to Mary, "If you are ready to give your life to Jesus, then I will find some others to pray with us."

I had learned that entrance into God's kingdom is a church matter. Since the angels rejoice and have a party when a sinner comes home, there should be a gathering on the local level. I found that if converts begin in the closet, they will probably continue to stay there rather than become a strong part of the church.

"Yes, I'm ready."

The glow was already there. One can always tell when the Holy Spirit is at work bringing new life to a person. Although we cannot predict the movement of the Holy Spirit, we can surely know when He is present. By His grace and power He revealed Jesus to this woman.

This is part of the meaning of the word given to the churches in Philadelphia and Laodicea. First, the door of the kingdom of God is open and no one can shut it. God's plan in Jesus Christ is to make sure that anyone whose heart is bent toward God can find his way into the kingdom. But more than that, God doesn't make the person go to Him; He comes right to the door of each heart: "Here I am! I stand at the door and knock. If anyone hears my voice and opens the door, I will come in and eat with him, and he with me" [Rev. 3:20].

God had gone right to the door of this woman's heart and had knocked. When she opened it, she could not resist the one who was standing before her—Jesus! There was only one thing to do and that was to help her invite Jesus into her life. This is what Scripture tells us: "Yet to all who received him, to those who believed in his name, he gave the right to become children of God" [John 1:12].

Church people often make up rules that others must follow before they are acceptable to God. You must pray this way, you must say this thing, and if you don't you won't get in. As a result, people are convinced that they must do something to merit getting into the kingdom. Rather than accepting all that God has prepared for them, they say something like, "I must get ready."

God's Gift of Grace Available to All

I marvel afresh that it is by grace that God saves people. It is His love that quiets the turbulent, deep waters of life. His love, which is poured out in Jesus Christ, has no restrictions. He never says to one person, "Now you can have my love," and to another, "But *you* can't." I groan inside when I realize we create barriers for people because we don't love in the same manner as God.

I was observing a living example of a sacrament in action. We define sacraments as "outward and visible signs of inward and spiritual grace."[1] Mary was visibly displaying the fact that an "inward and spiritual grace" was present in her life. She glowed with Jesus. The words of Paul became excitingly real to me. I could almost hear: "'The Word is near you; it is in your mouth and in your heart,' that is, the word of faith we are proclaiming: that if you confess with your mouth, 'Jesus is Lord,' and believe in your heart that God raised him from the dead, you will be saved. For it is with your heart that you believe and are justified, and it is with your mouth that you confess and are saved" [Rom. 10:8–10]. To see the living reality of God's word in action made my spirit soar.

The sacramental act was completed for this woman when she confessed with her mouth that which was being revealed in her heart. The Holy Spirit enabled her to go through the door and enter her life of salvation and to confess that Jesus is Lord. Not only did the Holy Spirit reveal and lead her to confess Jesus, but He also revealed other things for her to do to make her entry into the kingdom of God more sure.

God's Covenant Promise: A Relationship with Jesus

About six hundred years before Jesus was born, God promised that we could have a relationship with him; this was a covenant promise. "I will be their God and they will be my people. No longer will a man teach his neighbor, or a man his brother, saying 'Know the Lord,' because they will all know me, from the least of them to the greatest" [Jer. 31:33–34]. Only those who have been born into the family of God (the church) are able to experience being God's supernatural people. We become aware of this new nature when God comes into our lives and we surrender to him. As we embrace and are embraced by the power of the cross, our sinful old life is put to death and a new one is born. Paul described it this way, "When you were dead in your sins and in the uncircumcision of your sinful nature, God made you alive with Christ" [Col. 2:13]. Jesus said it more plainly, "No one can see the Kingdom of God unless he is born again" [John 3:3, NASB]. Fortunately for us, God's covenant promise is that we all can have a relationship with Jesus; we all can be part of God's kingdom.

There is nothing more personal than to have the God of the universe enter into your heart, searching to see if you are bent towards Him. Should He find such an inclination, He instructs His Holy Spirit to bring you into His family. If there is resistance, then one remains a natural person, unable to worship God in Spirit, unable to be part of His family. John said that "to all who receive him [Jesus], to those who believed in his name, he gave the right to become children of God—children born not of natural descent, nor of human decision or a husband's will, but born of God" [John 1:12–13].

It is not uncommon for people to be faithful to the church but to have no personal relationship with God. Their hearts may not yet be bent towards Him. Yet unless we turn to Jesus, new life will elude us. It is God's command that people everywhere repent and turn to Him so that they may be saved [see Acts 17:30; 26:18]. Everyone must enter into a personal relationship with God, so God can lead and guide him. This is not an intellectual relationship of a "Bible-less brain," but an experience with the living God. Knowledge does not save a person or make him a child of God—being born again does. Being born again is something we *experience* when the Holy Spirit fills us with His life-giving presence.

A Forgiving God

A second woman arrived, answering the call that I had made for someone to come and pray with Mary. The two women knew each other. Nancy, upon entering, could tell at first glance that God was at work. She embraced her newly born sister in Christ.

"Let's kneel at the altar rail and pray," I said, moving to the inside of the rail so I could face them. Nancy stayed beside the woman. "I'll pray for you now, asking that God will enable you, by the power of the Holy Spirit, to do all that you will need to do."

"I'm scared," Mary said softly. Indeed, she should have some fear, for she had come into the hands of the living God. But this is a good fear—the beginning of wisdom. I said, "Mary, you should be awed by what is happening, but don't let that stop you from responding to God." I continued by praying for her, "Father, thank you for the way in which your love has been poured into Mary's heart. I pray for her now that the power of Your Holy Spirit will enable her to know what to pray and how to do it. I ask this in the name of Jesus." Then no word was spoken for some time.

Mary began speaking, haltingly at first, and then with great fervency, "I'm . . . so . . . sorry . . . O God, how I am sorry for the life I have been living. I am sorry that I have been so unfaithful. I have sinned against you, Father. Forgive me, please forgive me." Tears flowed until it was difficult to understand what was being said through the sobs. "I give myself to you. I don't want to do those things again; I just want to be yours. Take me, Father, take me."

I made the sign of the cross on her forehead. "Mary, in the name of Jesus, in the name of the Father, Son, and Holy Spirit, I declare that your sins are forgiven. Receive this forgiveness into your heart and give thanks to God." Mary's eyes opened, and as she looked at me she radiated God's presence.

"O yes, Father, I do accept your forgiveness. Thank you, Father, thank you for loving me."

I always try to ascertain that those who come to the Lord have been freed from all darkness. I said, "Now, Mary, we always like to make sure you understand that you are coming away from the devil's kingdom of darkness, the one that has ruled your life for so long, and now you are entering the kingdom of God to receive all that God has stored up for you. Because of this, we like to encourage you to renounce all the devil's work, no matter how it may have affected you."

Out of Darkness and into the Light

"If you have ever been involved in the occult, then confess it and renounce it."

Mary looked at me with a question in her eyes.

I said, "Things like witchcraft, white or black, astrology, Jeanne Dixon and Edgar Cayce, spiritualism, fortune-telling, Ouija boards, and such."

There were a number of such things that she had been involved in, and quickly she set about to confess and renounce them.

"Now, ask Jesus to come into your life, since He has been knocking at your heart's door."

"Jesus, come into my life. You are my Lord, You are my Savior; be with me forever. Never leave me." Soon after that, Mary received the baptism in the Holy Spirit and began to speak in tongues. She was ecstatic for weeks.

This event is typical of scores that I experienced with people who had been lifelong pew warmers. They were like I was. I attended church but did not know God. There is a false assumption clergy often have: they feel that everyone who attends church is a Christian. Once, I met with a clergyman who had a parishioner who wrote down his disbelief. He said he didn't believe in the Resurrection, the virgin birth, or that Jesus is God. The clergyman was fearful of confronting the man with the truth. But I know that not to believe in the basic tenets of our faith is pagan.

Another troublesome assumption prevails in the Episcopal church— the belief that it is good Christian behavior not to pry into one's personal faith. "Religion is a personal matter." Nowadays, however, the opposite is true. We need to pry into people's Christian beliefs and discover whether or not we have a church left. We may be fooling ourselves into believing that religious people are necessarily Christian. Ideas of personal faith and personal conversion have been abandoned by much of today's church. And where faith has not been abandoned, the work of the Holy Spirit has, making evangelism a mere recitation of a catechism. Evangelism in some churches merely means a good canvass for pledges or an increase in church attendance.

Once I was in terrible darkness concerning matters of faith. Now I am coming into the light. I was never prepared to understand or to present the gospel to anyone until after that time when the Lord baptized me in the Holy Spirit. Before, I was in the darkness of believing that only worldly disciplines, such as psychology, psychiatry, sociology, and business, had anything to offer the individual. This was especially true of someone with a significant life problem.

Saved from Suicide

One day in my office I looked at the strained, haggard features of the woman before me.

"Why are you here?" I asked.

"Because my friend said I should talk with you."

"What do you need to be talking about?"

"I guess it's because I have been thinking about suicide, about killing myself."

"Things are not going well in your life?" I was already praying that the Lord would give me something supernatural to use—a gift of his Holy Spirit. Without God's help, I believed I would be unable to help this woman. A few years ago, I would have had her in a psychiatrist's office before the day was over. This was the way I was taught in seminary. There were certain "cases," I was told, that needed "professional" help, lest we hurt someone.

"No, they aren't," her voice trailed off as she stared at her hands.

"Is it your marriage?"

"It's everything. Nothing is right about my life. My husband is running around with another woman; he's been doing that all of our married life. My children are gone; their lives are really messed up. They think I should leave him."

"What about you, personally? What's happening inside of you when you are home alone?"

"I seem to sleep all of the time. I feel so depressed. Nothing I do seems to help. I should just end it all; then, I could get some rest, some peace." I saw the dark circles under her eyes which told of sleepless nights.

"Have you been to a doctor for a physical?'

"Yes, but he just said that I needed some psychiatric help. He did give me some pills to take."

"Are you taking them?"

"They make me so drowsy, and anyhow, they don't really help."

"What about the psychiatrist?"

"I went to one about six months ago. He just told me that I should leave my husband and do something positive in my life."

"How often have you thought about suicide?"

"Many times recently."

"If you were going to do it, how would you do it?"

"I've saved up some pills at home."

"Why haven't you done it yet?"

"I don't know." This answer showed me that she was serious: she knew how she was going to do it, and there was no good reason preventing her.

"What is your relationship with Jesus?" This was becoming one of my stock-in-trade questions, for there is nothing more important when a person is in trouble than her relationship with God.

"I've prayed, and prayed and prayed. God just doesn't answer my prayers." Her response revealed that she had no relationship with God. She knew how to call out to Him, but she wasn't hearing an answer.

"What do you think will happen to you if you kill yourself?"

"If God is loving, then He should understand. He knows that I need some rest and peace in my life."

"Murder is a sin, you know."

"But it isn't the same. I just need some rest. If I kill myself, then it will be over. I won't have to go through this anymore."

"If you kill yourself, you will not have any rest." Suddenly, I was getting the word of wisdom that I needed; God was answering my prayer for help. "The devil is the father of lies. He is the one who is telling you that you will have peace if you kill yourself. He is waiting for you to follow his word so he can have you forever. After you kill yourself, you will belong to the devil, and with him there will never be peace, only torment, and worse torment than you have yet experienced."

I had her interest. "But God is loving and he wouldn't let that happen to me."

"You wouldn't be obeying God; you would be obeying the devil. If you abandon God, He will abandon you. Scripture says, 'If we disown him, he will also disown us' [2 Tim. 2:12b]. Jesus has power over death to life, if you choose Him. Then He will not let you kill yourself. There is only one way for you. You must choose Jesus and God's kingdom. He will enter your life and show you how to live, right now."

I could tell that the Holy Spirit had begun to work in her heart, so I continued, "If you invite Jesus to come into your life, it won't be to solve your problems. What God promises is that He will give you a new life. He will come into your heart and change you forever. He will require, however, that you repent. That means surrender your entire life to Jesus with a resolve not to take up ownership again, not even of your problems. God will fill you with hope, faith, and love. Then you will know what to do with the circumstances of your life."

"That's what I want. I want God in my life, but I don't know how to make it happen."

"You can't make it happen, but God can and will. All He is interested in is your heart, whether it's open to Him or not."

"I want Him in my life."

"I'll get some people to pray with us. I know that God will see that your heart's desire is fulfilled. The Holy Spirit causes you to have new life in the kingdom as you are born again. This comes by the grace of God and in His time."

Soon we had a group of people. The praying began and the woman, being touched by the Holy Spirit, gave her life to Jesus. She forgave all of the people who had hurt her. It was easy to see that the forgiveness was really a deliverance, a freeing of her soul from a deep bondage. The radiance of love began to come over her. Her face had changed from one of deep distress to one of joy.

She had come in with a heavy heart, despairing of life, and had found the living God who poured love into her heart. Then Jesus baptized her in the Holy Spirit, and she began to speak in tongues. Since that day, the woman has never been the same. The joy of the Lord was permanent. She now viewed her circumstances through different eyes. She no longer had the feelings that caused her to lose sleep; she was transformed—born again.

A Definition for Evangelism

Evangelism is the Holy Spirit-infused process [see Rom. 8:16; Gal. 4:6; 1 Cor. 2:13; Acts 13:2; 2 Cor. 3:6] whereby a person who is separated from Christ, excluded from God's family, severed from God's promises and hopelessly without God [see Eph. 2:12], is set free from the dark power of Satan's kingdom [see Acts 26:18], and brought into the hope, promise, and liberty of the family of God through the blood that Jesus Christ shed on the Cross [see Eph 2:13]. Evangelism finds its completion when a person is born again of the Spirit [see John 3:3–8, 1:13; Titus 3:5; 1 Peter 1:23; 2 Cor. 5:17], made a disciple of Jesus Christ [see Matt. 28:18–20, 16:24; Luke 14:26, 33; John 8:31, 15:8], and brought to maturity in Christ [see Eph. 4:13–24; 1 Cor. 13:11; Heb. 5:14].

Evangelism is performed when Christians become witnesses [see Acts 1:4–5, 8] for Jesus Christ by giving testimony of their experience of and relationship with Him and of their fellowship with those who share in that relationship [see 1 John 1:1–3]. The open doors for evangelizing people and the power for making it happen are provided by the Holy Spirit [see Col. 4:3–4; Mark 16:20; 1 Cor. 2:4–5; Rom. 15:18–19; Acts 4:33, 5:12; 6:8, 8:6, 14:3].

Three Important Gifts

Church renewal begins with the people who are church members. Failure to reach out to them will result in a slowing or stopping of renewal. My seminary did not teach this fact. The Lord gave me three gifts to better understand the renewal that was going on at St. Luke's.

The first gift was *a deep understanding and conviction that until a person is reconciled to God, there is no true meaning or purpose for his life.*

The second gift was *an understanding that very few baptized and confirmed mainline church members have any relationship with the Lord.*

The third, related to the first two, was *a deep, unrestrained desire to see the entire congregation come into a relationship with God.* These three gifts came to me early and, I believe, made church renewal at St. Luke's possible. I knew that I had to begin by evangelizing the congregation. After a time, all but a few members of St. Luke's claimed they knew the Lord and were filled with the Holy Spirit.

Most counselors whom I know believe that the initial sessions with a counselee should be spent on a discovery process; they try to uncover a person's real problems and they look for root causes. Once a diagnosis is made, they then try to offer logical solutions. That's the way I used to do it, but after the Lord filled me with His Holy Spirit, I learned that there is a better way to begin. When I discovered that only God can heal a troubled person, I knew that it was necessary to lead people to Him first. Then I learned that unless a person receives help from God, everything else is temporary. Only God's healing has lasting effect and meaning. The solution is simple: find out what a person's relationship with God is. And if there is none, or a poor one at best, then there is no reason to continue counseling until there is a relationship established.

The deep problems of life, such as alcoholism, divorce, adultery, homosexuality, abortion, and depression are spiritual problems first and social and psychological problems second. Although the world is able to help people sometimes, God is able to heal them. Since these are spiritual problems, we first go to God through Jesus. I say, "Tell me, how would you describe your relationship with Jesus?"

"Why do you ask that question?" they often ask.

"Well, you have come to me for help with a problem that you have. I want to be as helpful as I am able, but I personally have so little to offer.

There is only one Healer for our life situations, and that is Jesus. If I am to be of help, then we must go to Him, surrender and seek His guidance. If your relationship with Jesus is not very good, then the first thing that I must do is help you get one. Would you be willing to go with me to God for help?"

"But all I wanted was some advice. Do we have to go through all that right now?"

"I'm sorry, but I have nothing to offer you except what God has to offer. If you are willing to trust God for solutions, then I am here to help. If you feel that you cannot, then I know some excellent psychologists to whom I can refer you."

Although this, to some, sounds rather harsh, I believe that it is the most loving response to someone in need. Peter said to the lame man, ". . . Silver or gold I do not have, but what I have I give you. . ." [Acts 3:6]. I believe that to offer someone temporary solutions to life's problems is not very loving. But to offer the Lord first and other solutions later gives people the best that there is available. Besides, the counseling office is a great place to evangelize people.

The Doorway to Jesus

The Holy Spirit is the doorway to a relationship with Jesus Christ. This is the Father's plan that Jesus revealed. "But when he, the Spirit of truth, comes, he will guide you into all truth. . . . He will bring glory to me by taking from what is mine and making it known to you" [John 16:13–14]. If anything life-changing is revealed to us, the only source of that revelation will be the Holy Spirit. Often, as we grow up in mainline churches, we are deprived spiritually. When this happens, we will find it difficult to understand the things that the Holy Spirit reveals. "The man without the Spirit does not accept the things that come from the Spirit of God, for they are foolishness to him, and he cannot understand them, because they are spiritually discerned" [1 Cor. 2:14].

Mainline seminaries generally do not teach students how to discern the things of the Spirit. If they learn how, they must do it either before they enter seminary or after they graduate. It seems strange that this is so when *everything that God does is by the work and operation of the Holy Spirit.* To be without some understanding of the reality of the Holy Spirit is the same as being without God. It is important for clergy to understand things about the Holy Spirit since they are called to help others discern the movement and activity of the Spirit. It is especially significant since the Holy Spirit provides us with our only access to God Himself.

The work of the Holy Spirit is a very personal one; He knows who we are and seeks us personally. In His personal way, He reveals Jesus to our hearts. Although the church is a corporate body, entry into it is still personal. The Holy Spirit opens the door to the kingdom of God for each of us by introducing us to Jesus. As we believe in Him and receive Him, we become the Father's children. The fact of this personal relationship with God was promised by the prophet Jeremiah [see Jer. 31:34]. Though it was promised, people are often surprised to discover that it is true. They were never taught that a personal relationship with God is very important, and, in fact, essential to full Christian life. It is the Holy Spirit who confirms whether we have this relationship or not [see Rom. 8:16].

When we took teams of laypeople from St. Luke's Church to do ministry in other churches beginning in renewal, the question about one's relationship with God was always an important one. While in small groups, we asked people to answer the question, "On a scale of zero to ten, what is your relationship with Jesus Christ?" Most answered between zero and five. It was a startling discovery to hear faithful Episcopalians declaring their spiritual poverty. They didn't have a relationship with God! The ironic part of their poverty was that we were usually the first people to tell them that a relationship with God is possible.

The Power of God at Work

Paul said this: "My message and my preaching were not with wise and persuasive words, but with a demonstration of the Spirit's power, so that your faith might not rest on men's wisdom, but on God's power" [1 Cor. 2:4–5]. After I was baptized in the Holy Spirit, I discovered that evangelism was easy. It became a matter of following the Holy Spirit's lead—going where He was going and emulating what He was doing. I had to learn to cease operating in my own strength and to start depending on His. The Holy Spirit became my principal teacher and guide when it came to evangelism. Once we learn that business, industry, psychological techniques, education, and sociology cannot replace God, we are on our way toward being evangelists. This is not a matter of being anti-intellectual, as some will say, but one of putting first things first, of being obedient to God. Anything less is anti-God. Should we ever declare that the world's answers to life's questions are better than God's, then we are against Him.

In order to learn to evangelize others, we must learn to understand things the way the Holy Spirit understands them. We must recognize that God's ways are always best and that the world has no power to bring people into a relationship with Him. If God wishes to use the things of the world to draw people to Himself, then He must show that way. Otherwise, we will fail to see what the Holy Spirit is doing, or wanting to do, and people will not be converted to Jesus Christ. Evangelism is a spiritual exercise; it is God's word put to work. It is a spiritual transaction—one kingdom for another [see Acts 26:16–18]. It is the Holy Spirit who convinces people that Jesus is truly the Son of God and that His death on the cross means something for them personally. It is the Holy Spirit who tells people that they must believe in Jesus and give themselves totally to Him. It is the Holy Spirit who teaches people to "worship the Father in Spirit and in truth" [John 4:24]. It is only the Holy Spirit who is able to teach one person how to love another. "The Spirit searches all things, even the deep things of God" [1 Cor. 2:10].

It is possible for people to mount up great evangelistic campaigns that God never intended to bless. Instead of following the leading of the Holy Spirit, they do what they want to do. Often they end up coaxing people into the kingdom. The general result of coaxing people into the kingdom is that they have to be coaxed to stay.

Often, I have heard conversations such as this:

"I just don't feel anything." (The person has just finished praying something they were told to pray.)

"You don't feel anything? Well, don't worry, the kingdom of God is not built on feelings."

"But I'm not sure," the person is almost pleading.

"Don't worry about it. God's word has said it. Just believe it; that's all you need to do."

This awful ministry makes entrance into the kingdom a matter of pushing the right buttons on the elevator. Sometime later the person returns.

"I just don't feel good anymore since I became a Christian."

"That's negative thinking. Just hang on to the fact that you prayed the prayer; don't be ruled by your feelings. Have faith. Just keep reading and confessing the word."

43

The Holy Spirit has not done the work, and this person knows it. The evangelist, however, cannot see the facts and ends up trying to make the person please him by saying the "right" things.

Unless a person's heart is convinced by the Holy Spirit, the act of repeating prayers is merely an empty exercise, for he will look at you and tell you that nothing has happened. You will have to tell the person to accept it on faith, which he never really had in the beginning. He will end up being guilty or disappointed, believing that God does not care. This all may happen because the evangelist failed to listen to the Holy Spirit and the person. When a person is born again, he will know it; he will not have to be convinced.

I was asked once to counsel with a woman who had come from a very prominent Christian community. She was in deep trouble emotionally, and although she had received ministry by a Christian psychiatrist for a couple of years, her life had not changed.

"Tell me about your life," I said to the woman. I had heard so much advance material that I wanted to hear it directly from her. She began to tell me the tale of woe that had troubled her for years. She told how she had found her way to the community and how the people there had ministered to her.

As I was listening, I was asking the Lord for insight. The Lord was quick to give me the answer, "She doesn't know me."

"Tell me, what is your relationship with the Lord?" She just looked at me blankly. "You don't really have one, do you?"

Tears welled up in her eyes, and she shook her head no. Soon she began to unfold the story about how she arrived at the community, not knowing anything about the Lord, and how she finally entered into a household. The leaders assumed that she had a relationship with the Lord. As a result of this miscalculation, they applied spiritual principles to her life that had no ultimate meaning. She never told them otherwise because she didn't want to disappoint them.

I presented the gospel to her, giving her Scripture and testimony. The Lord had already begun to work in her heart; she was ready to hear every word. I could see her changing. Finally, I asked her what the Lord was speaking to her heart. The answer was quite clear: God wanted her life. He wanted her to surrender to Him, for He loved her! Finally, I asked her if she would like to pray, completing the sacramental act. After we gathered a group of people, we prayed with her. Soon all was complete, and she began to radiate God's presence.

Sometimes those who are evangelizing others spend a lot of time giving the word. But when the word has been given they may fail to follow up on what the Holy Spirit has done in the person's heart. They may fail to pop the question: "Can I pray with you?" Often, when people have heard God speak to their hearts, they do not know what to do next. Unless someone helps them, they are often left hanging. They heard the Holy Spirit say, "Come," but do not know where or how. It is the responsibility of the evangelist to hear what the Holy Spirit is doing and to be a harvester by asking a person to make a response.

Good salespeople make use of three principles:

One, they must know the product well.

Two, they must be willing to make the call on a prospect.

Three, they must be willing to ask the person to buy.

With evangelism it is much the same. It is essential that we know Jesus before we can make Him known to others. We must be willing to risk making the call on people, to introduce them to the Lord. We must be willing to pray with people so that they actually receive what is being promised.

Only One Way to God

Because we have problems to solve is not the reason for seeking God. We seek God because we are disconnected from the source of true and eternal life without Him. We need God because we are prisoners of the world, the flesh, and the devil without Him. But we cannot be with God unless we are provided a way to get to Him. There is only one way that God has provided: that is through Jesus Christ. That way is made possible because of His death on the cross and His resurrection from the dead. Without passing through Jesus, even church members will be without God's life.

Many church people are sincere, religious persons, but very poor Christians. They cannot be faulted in their willingness, for they desire to do all that the church requires of them (and that is very little). Many have served over the years in nearly every capacity that is available. Despite their heroic efforts to do good things, they are in spiritual poverty, having no relationship with God.

Many times, after hearing me say things such as this, people accused me of being judgmental or fanatic. The Lord, however, has shown me that this is loving judgment, for it has the most important concern in mind for the people—their relationship with God. God's first act of loving was to give us Jesus. Ours should be also. We have to love people enough that we will give them Jesus even if they don't want Him. Failure to present Jesus to a congregation is a failure to love them. All other acts of charity pale before that one great act of love, "Do you know Jesus?"

We can always trust that the Holy Spirit has gone before us when we are presenting Jesus to someone. But since our ministry should be obedient to the Holy Spirit's direction, then it is best to seek His guidance as to our next assignment. It is always easier that way. When we follow the Holy Spirit about, then we harvest, not plow.

Paul talked about evangelism in terms of the open door [see 1 Cor. 16:8-9). The Holy Spirit can lead us to the open doors, to the places where He has been preparing grace for people. "And pray for us, too, that God may open a door for our message, so that we may proclaim the mystery of Christ . . ." [Col. 4:3]. Paul also understood that evangelism is not some system that a Christian works out, but that the message given at the particular time needs to be inspired. "Pray that I may proclaim it clearly as I should" [Col. 4:3-4].

Three Basic Conversions

Leaders of congregations will find their work much easier if they recognize the need for each individual to experience three major conversions. First, the definition of conversion that I prefer is offered by the theologian, C. B. Moss: "Conversion is the conscious turning of the soul to God."[2] Surrender to God is essential if one is to participate in and enjoy the benefits of God's kingdom. The surrendering of one's self to God may be a sudden decision made after an experience of the presence of God, or it may be something that happened over a period of time. But for it to be a conversion, a surrender must take place. If one has surrendered to God, then that person will definitely know it.

The three conversions are:

1. *Conversion to Jesus Christ* (and by implication, conversion to the supernatural kingdom life into which one is reborn).
2. *Conversion to the Church* (and by implication, conversion to the church's supernatural life within the kingdom of God).
3. *Conversion to Ministry* (and by implication, conversion to the supernatural ministry of the church as coworkers with God and with God's people).

Each conversion is important, not only to the individual, but to the church as a whole. A church does not grow in Christ unless its people have surrendered their lives to Jesus Christ. A church cannot get fellowship going until the people are converted to the church. A church cannot get ministry going until the people are converted to ministry.

Conversion to Jesus Christ

One of the most damaging assumptions that we can make about church people is that they are converted to Jesus. In this day it serves the church better when *we assume members are not converted to Jesus Christ unless they say otherwise.* C. B. Moss helps us again. We may begin, he stresses, a life of grace at our baptism, but this does not automatically "develop into spiritual life."[3] In the same way, baptism, though it *testifies* to the forgiveness of sins, does not remove the tendency to sin. The remedy is conversion, which brings one into a relationship with God and makes sure the process of regeneration.

True conversion begins in the heart of the person. "For it is with your heart that you believe and are justified . . ." [Rom. 10:10]. The seeds of conversion are planted in our hearts when the Holy Spirit reveals Jesus to us, when the Word of God is spoken internally, and when we find ourselves drawn to Him. This may happen to us before or after our baptism. In either case, our *salvation is not secure* until we are individually drawn to Jesus Christ. This is why godparents, parents, and the church bear such a weighty responsibility when they baptize infants.

When we are converted to Jesus Christ, our outlook for the future will begin to change. We will find reading the Bible a joy, filling our lives with new understandings about Jesus. We will want to become faithful disciples of Jesus. The leaders, however, will have to keep their eyes on us, because our conversion to Jesus last night will not make us be today's perfect disciples. It takes time. We must be patient, and our leaders must be patient with us.

We may be helped on our way to obedience to Christ by answering this question: "If Jesus is truly Lord, then. . . ." Just fill in the blanks. "I must," "We must," "The committee I serve on must," etc. We can pray and consider what must change if Jesus is actually Lord. Once we begin to consider such an important Christian foundation stone, then our lives and the life of our church will begin to change. Without the opportunity to be converted to Christ, none of these considerations will be made.

Evangelism, therefore, must continue in and out of the church. It reaches in to the members who yet need to be converted to Jesus Christ, and it reaches out to the community and world to win others to Christ. Evangelism within the church is of extreme importance since it prepares the church body to receive outsiders. Here are some ideas about how to evangelize those within and without the Church:

1. *Interviews with members.* As we keep records about baptisms, confirmations, marriages, etc., statistics also need to be maintained concerning the three conversions of the members. The most adequate manner of gathering this information from the members is through an interview process. Here, learning to ask the proper questions is a must. "What is your relationship with Jesus Christ?" "Can you tell me about the time when you surrendered your life to Jesus Christ?" "Jesus valued the church more than most Christians probably do. Can you describe your commitment to the fellowship of the church?" "I notice that you have not yet been given the opportunity to do ministry. Is there some aspect of Christian ministry toward which you are being drawn?" There is nothing judgmental about this process as long as you take people's answers at face value. This information will help you concentrate your evangelistic efforts properly.

2. *Evangelism training.* Teach your leaders how to do practical evangelism. This training must include how to present the gospel of Jesus Christ from the Bible, how to be effective in giving personal testimony, how to pray with people to receive Christ, how to pray for people to receive the baptism in the Holy Spirit, and how to disciple those who have consciously turned their lives over to Jesus Christ. Since it is quite possible for a church not to have leaders who are able to teach evangelism, it is prudent to discover congregations that are being successful in their evangelism and ask those people for teaching help.

3. *Books and tapes.* People who are targeted for evangelism need to be reading and listening to inspirational material. Tapes of personal testimonies and books describing how God changed someone's life are especially helpful. After people

have read or listened to the material, a follow-up can be made to pray with them. Two of the most effective books on the market are *Nine O'Clock in the Morning* by Dennis Bennett and *Basic Christianity* by John Stott.

4. *Conferences.* Renewal conferences provide a venue for people to be won to Christ. It is best if large groups from your church can be encouraged to attend. It is always worth the effort to use every means to encourage those who need to be evangelized. This is a place for leaders to be bold. The more people who experience the same thing, the more breakthroughs will happen and the more people will be willing to be converted to the church.

5. *Renewal weekends.* Plan renewal weekends for your church, bringing experts from other congregations to do the teaching and evangelizing. Tell the leaders what you wish to happen at the weekend, and then give them a free hand to do as God leads. Give responsibilities for the weekend to those who need to be evangelized. Do everything in your power to get people to attend. Be sure that the most influential people conduct a telephone campaign to encourage attendance.

6. *Cursillo.* Cursillo weekends are available in both the Roman Catholic and Episcopal churches. Cursillo weekends have proven to be very effective in evangelizing people. They seem to be able to inspire some of the more difficult cases. However, the church should have its own process for follow-up that will immediately begin to disciple the newly converted.

7. *Saints Alive.* Conduct "Saints Alive" classes three times a year. Make them a requirement for new members and transfers. In addition, target those who need to be evangelized. This material, from England, is available through Episcopal Renewal Ministries. The teaching is basic Christianity. The aim is to lead people to Christ and see them baptized in the Holy Spirit.

8. *Life in the Spirit.* "Life in the Spirit" courses are very similar to the "Saints Alive." With very insightful presentations, people are led to make a commitment to Jesus Christ and to be filled with the Holy Spirit. Both courses can easily be led by laypeople.

9. *Neighborhood Bible studies.* Teach your leaders how to conduct evangelistic Bible studies. Then, have those who need to

be evangelized act as hosts for a four-week effort. Not only can you reach the unchurched, but the host is also a captive audience. Some of the typical materials covered are: "Who is Jesus Christ?" "Why did God send Jesus to save us?" "What is the meaning of the Cross and Resurrection?" "How can I receive all that God planned for me?"

10. *Child evangelism.* Make child evangelism the primary and overriding aim of church schools, Sunday schools, and youth groups. Young people from about four years old and up can be led to Christ, receive the Baptism in the Holy Spirit and learn how to be effective members of the church. No one who is yet to be converted should be made a church member. Part of the training would include how to lead others to Christ, how to pray with others for healing, and how to read the Bible.

11. *Altar calls every Sunday.* Good sermons often leave people in the lurch by providing them with no opportunity to respond. Sermons that do not offer prayer opportunities may automatically become poor sermons. The best solution is an altar call, allowing those being touched by God to come and receive prayer. If congregational sensitivities prevent an altar call directly following the sermon, then opportunities can be given immediately after people receive Communion. Have prayer teams ready to pray with those who were stirred by the sermon or for any other reason.

12. *Prayer and praise meetings.* Weekly prayer and praise meetings provide a consistent time and place for someone to hear about and to receive Jesus Christ. These meetings are usually events of high spiritual impact and are perfect for evangelizing some people. Meeting contents vary, but a typical meeting begins with the singing of newer praise and worship songs, verbal praise and prayer. This might be followed with several testimonies about what God has been doing in certain lives. Then include the reading of Scripture and a sermon/teaching. This is followed with an altar call. Then sing and praise to bring the meeting to a close. At the close of the meeting there could be a general time of people praying for one another.

13. *Cell groups or house churches.* Cell groups or house churches are best when they are formed to reach out and receive new people. They provide a place for people to praise

God, hear His word, hear testimony of God's acts and pray for any need. They are also an excellent place for discipling people, keeping them focused on the parish vision, and serving God's will. Cell groups are designed to be small, thus providing an intimate setting for the timid.

Conversion to the Church

Church leaders are often mystified because those who are converted to Jesus Christ do not participate in church activities. These persons, though claiming great personal relationships with God, express no need for participation in anything but Sunday services. A usual reason for such responses is that the people have yet to be converted to the church. They usually cannot recognize the body of Christ. It is very important for Christians not only to recognize the body of Christ but to understand their part in it. Paul remarked, "Is not the bread that we break a participation in the body of Christ? Because there is one loaf, we, who are many, are one body, for we all partake of the one loaf" [1 Cor. 10:16–17].

We all participate in the body of Christ if we belong to Christ. It is a family arrangement that we cannot avoid, even if we wish to. When John described this, he talked about inviting others to "have fellowship with us" [1 John 1:3]. Paul warned us of the grave consequences when we fail to recognize the body of Christ [see 1 Cor. 11:27–30].

Conversion to the church occurs when the Holy Spirit enables a person to see the body of Christ through God's eyes. Once seeing its significance in God's eyes, each person is given the opportunity to commit his life to the church. This is an "all for one and one for all" understanding. In the early church it meant having everything in common, as well as meeting together daily [see Acts 2:42–47]. The conversion to the church is a real conversion that is spurred by good teaching and confirmed by the Holy Spirit.

When people are converted to the church, a likely consequence will be tithing to the local church body. Not only will those people begin to tithe to the church, but they will also willingly come under the authority of its leaders. In this sense the people are becoming more like what God wants. They begin doing God's work by offering their talents, experience, and supernatural gifts to the building up of God's body. In addition, newly converted people will welcome being included in small weekly fellowship groups.

Conversion to Jesus Christ is difficult to measure by observation since it begins inwardly and works itself outwardly. Conversions to the church, however, can be seen in the actions of the people. They act out their conversions by participating in the full life of the local body. It is rather easy for leaders, therefore, to keep track of those who have been converted in this manner.

Here are five ways to help get people converted to the church:

1. *Saints Together.* This teaching series is designed to help people form small groups and ground them in basics about relationships. This material, published in England, is available through Episcopal Renewal Ministries.

2. *Called and Committed.* Hold special classes taught from the book *Called and Committed* by David Watson. This book is probably the best written for a community growing in the Lord. It is very useful for teaching.

3. *Teaching on Sunday morning.* Bring an evangelist to preach on Sunday morning concerning our need to be converted to the church. This preaching should be followed by an altar call inviting people to turn their lives over to God through His church.

4. *Cell Groups.* A useful guide to the development of cell groups can be found in the book *Where Do We Go From Here?* by Ralph W. Neighbor. This book contains just about all one might need to understand and begin these small groups.

5. *The Gospel Conspiracy Workbook.* This book by Charles Irish is designed to be used with a book called *The Gospel Conspiracy* by Michael Marshall. The usefulness of the workbook is to help churches form small groups, begin to study the Bible, learn to pray with one another, and deepen relationships.

Conversion to Ministry

Many clergy have been unable to solve the mystery of why they are unable to get people to participate in the ministry of the church. For instance, they hold classes about evangelism but cannot get the people to do it. The answer is simple: they are not yet converted to ministry. When people are converted to ministry, they will see the imperative in their hearts. They respond to a longing in their hearts to fulfill God's will by serving others. If the longing is to evangelize people, they will see that they are called to bring life to people who live in death. If it is feeding and caring for the poor, they will burn with compassion that can only be satisfied when they fulfill God's will in this way. As it is difficult to push a wet noodle, so it is most difficult to get God's people to do ministry that is not in their hearts.

Proclaiming Jesus: The Mission of the Church

Proclaiming Jesus is a natural consequence for those who praise and worship Him.[4] If you know Him, then you will want to share Him with the world. Spreading the good news of Jesus Christ is something converted people willingly do. There is no way for the world to know about Him unless enthusiastic disciples make Him known. The church at Pentecost did not waste any time before making converts to Jesus Christ, with three thousand turning their lives over to God the first day. "The first Christians knew that they were all ambassadors of Christ, and wherever they went they 'gossiped the gospel.' It was not the apostles, the 'professionals,' but the ordinary nameless Christians who first brought the gospel to Rome."[5]

If one's relationship with the Lord means anything at all, it means that love must be shared with others. "We love because he first loved us" [1 John 4:19]. The burning desire of all true Christians is that the salvation in which they partake should be shared with all who will receive it. We evangelize others because "God has poured out his love into our hearts by the Holy Spirit, whom he has given us" [Rom. 5:5].

Today, millions are hungering for the assurance of God. They want to know if He still saves, if He still makes His presence known to people, and if He still transforms lives. Our missionary verve must become rekindled so that we satisfy the longing souls. An Episcopal bishop of Ohio, William Leonard, in an 1893 lecture, offered this thought that could have been written for today: "Men are anxiously asking today for a way that is both tried and assured—tried by the experience of the ages—whose path is well worn with pilgrim feet, whose direction is unmistakable. They want something positive—something in which they may place entire and unquestioning confidence—some rock that has withstood the shock of the billows and tides of unbelief, in the great sea of time."[6] We, of course, know the "rock" as Jesus Christ, crucified, resurrected, and ascended.

During the first four years of my ordained ministry, I was never to see a fresh convert to Jesus Christ. Some people were converted to the church but none to God. During the four years following my baptism in the Holy Spirit, I saw hundreds of converts to Jesus Christ. I was compelled to tell others about Him. The harvest was truly plentiful.

Feeding the Poor: The Mission of the Church

A second part of the church's mission is that of caring for the poor and oppressed. Any neglect of those who suffer in the world is a neglect of God Himself [see Matt. 25:31–46]. The writer of Hebrews was quick to add to his comment about praise with this: "And do not forget to do good and to share with others, for with such sacrifices God is pleased" [Heb. 13:16]. Cardinal Suenens said that "we have to learn how to integrate prayer and political action, prayer and social responsibility, prayer and justice, prayer and peace, prayer and the reconciliation of men."[7]

This work of caring for the poor and oppressed, however, cannot go on without the proclamation of the good news of the kingdom of God. This proclamation has its own power and does not need staff, bag, bread, clothes, or money [see Luke 9:3]. The food of the gospel will bring life and will last. "Man does not live on bread alone but on every word that comes from the mouth of the LORD" [Deut. 8:3]. It is a spiritual trap to assume that good works will produce converts to Jesus Christ through some sort of spin-off. "The very absurdity of treating Christian conversion as a byproduct of fruitful social welfare work underlines the converse point that social welfare work is in fact an inevitable byproduct of Christian conversion. Wherever the gospel of the resurrection has been preached and heard, hospitals have been built and the poor fed."[8] We must be careful lest we "are tempted to put our faith in parentheses, or to soft-pedal it in order to work better alongside others in the accomplishment of some goal."[9]

After a number of years of making new converts, I began to see that we were doing only half of the gospel-spreading work. We were bringing people into God's kingdom, but we weren't caring for the physically poor and oppressed. Our church, however, situated in the suburbs, was not a good venue for doing work among the needy. So that we could do this ministry better, we established a congregation in a poor ghetto in the inner city of Akron, full of those who have been beaten down in life. We knew that this work was necessary if we were to be faithful to Matthew 25 in a very direct way.

7

CONFRONTING THE DEMONIC

A Devilish Prayer Group

One of my seminary classmates phoned not too long after the Holy Spirit began to change the lives of some members of my congregation.

"Would you be willing to come over to Niles and speak to a prayer group in our church?"

I was not used to being bold with spiritual things, so it was with some apprehension that I agreed to do it.

When the evening arrived and Jan and I began our hour-and-a-half drive to Niles, we could feel that this was a very special trip. We had song sheets with us, so all the way there we sang the praise and worship songs that we had been learning. In between, we would pray that God would work His will through us. I have often looked back at that time of preparation as a very awesome moment with the Lord.

Nothing seemed out of the ordinary when we arrived at the host's home. The eleven people who had gathered were all nice enough, making us feel very welcome. The rector of the church for some reason was not able to be there—I guessed he was dealing with a crisis somewhere. There was also one member of the prayer group who could not attend.

"Could you tell me what your group has been doing?" I asked. I was interested in finding out if they knew much about the baptism in the Holy Spirit.

"We have been studying some books by Edgar Cayce," one of them offered.

The hair rose on the back of my neck; I was horrified. Among the things that are an absolute must when leading people to Christ and the fullness of the Holy Spirit is that they renounce their involvement with the occult. Not only that, but we have them renounce the devil himself. I was in the middle of the devil's den! It was a good thing that Jan and I had our hour-and-a-half preparation on the way over.

It was clear at that moment that just as I didn't know who they were, they didn't know who I was. I suppose that they thought I was there to bless their involvement with Edgar Cayce. I had thought they were some sort of Christian prayer group.

I remember when Dennis Bennett came to our church to help us better understand the work and operation of the Holy Spirit. When it came time for people to pray and receive Christ and the baptism in the Holy Spirit, he stopped for a time to explain the requirement that people renounce the occult.

"You will need to renounce any occult involvement, no matter how casual—things like Jeanne Dixon, Edgar Cayce, Ruth Montgomery, witchcraft, whether white or black, horoscopes, Ouija boards, seances, fortune-telling, palm reading, spiritism, and the like," Dennis exhorted.

In a few seconds after hearing the person say that they were reading Edgar Cayce, I made up my mind to take the offensive. The people were either going to throw us out of the house or were going to repent of their occult involvement.

"I am here to tell you that what you are doing is wrong. It is un-Christian and against the Word of God. Edgar Cayce is part of the occult and the occult does things through the devil's power, not God's." I continued, "Let me read what God's Word has to say about such things." I then turned to Deuteronomy 18:10.

"'Let no one be found among you who . . . practices divination [fortune-telling] or sorcery [incantations], interprets omens [foretelling, astrology], engages in witchcraft [calling on spirits for good or evil], or casts spells [hypnotism], or who is a medium [consults familiar spirits] or spiritist [possessed by a spirit guide, new age] or who consults the dead. Anyone who does these things is detestable to the LORD'" (brackets mine).

Then I read from 1 John 3:8. "The reason the Son of God appeared was to destroy the devil's work." Its impact on the people was obvious. They were like children who had been caught with their hands in the cookie jar. I surmised at that moment that their rector didn't really know what they were involved in.

Now that I had their attention, I continued to press on. "I can tell you didn't know that what you are doing is wrong in God's eyes. There is something, however, that you can do about it. But before I tell you what that is, let me tell you what has happened to me and what is happening in our church."

With that I gave them my own personal testimony, beginning with my discouragement and ending with the visit of Marilyn and Gig Korver. I told them how I finally surrendered my life to God and how I was filled with the Holy Spirit and began to speak in tongues. Then I told them about what was happening with the people in the church.

By this time they were all so quiet that you could have heard a pin drop on the carpet. "You too can have the same experience of God. In fact, God is knocking at the door of your hearts, seeking an invitation to come in and reside. He says in His Word that those who will believe in His name and receive Him into their lives will be transformed, or born again, to be His children."

I wasn't as confident in my heart as I was on the surface. I was hoping that they would respond favorably, but I didn't know. Now I had to go for broke—put it all on the line.

"Jan and I are going down to your church. We will wait there. If any of you know that you must renounce the occult and receive Christ into your hearts, then come and we will pray with you." I thought that a change of location would be better for their decision making process.

Satan Loses His Grip

All the way to the church Jan and I prayed hard, hoping that someone would show up. We went in, knelt at the altar rail, and waited. Then we heard the door open and the shuffling of feet. They had come! In fact, the entire group had come to the church! I began, "First, I want you to pray to the Lord out loud and tell Him why you are here in the church. I want you to understand that it is with your heart that you believe and are justified, and it is with your mouth that you confess and are saved." I continued with great confidence, for they had all begun to pray. "Now renounce any involvement that you have had with the occult; renounce the devil and all his works." In earnest, they renounced what they had been involved in.

"Many of you have been involved in sinful things, and in the secrets of your hearts you know what. Take time now to confess your sin to the Lord, telling Him that you are sorry and that you would like to be forgiven." As they prayed, tears fell down the cheeks of some.

"Before we can be set totally free, so that we can receive God's forgiveness, it is necessary that we forgive anyone who has wronged us in the past. Remember that Jesus told us that if we do not forgive men their sins, our Father will not forgive your sins. Let's recall those who have hurt us in any way, not worrying if they will ever repent. Think of their names. Now, let's begin, all together, I forgive _____ and _____. Please Lord, forgive me for holding things against them."

The big moment had arrived. "Now invite Jesus to come into your heart, into your life. Ask Him to be your savior and life-giver. Tell Him that you will make Him the Lord of your life from this day forward." I could see the faces change as God's radiance filled them.

Next, I explained about receiving the baptism in the Holy Spirit and about releasing the language of the Holy Spirit. I told them how they could have a spirit to Spirit communication with God. Then they prayed and received.

Just as I was finishing, the door of the church opened and Chuck, the rector, came in. As if he were drawn by the Lord, he walked straight to where we were praying, knelt down, and received the baptism of the Holy Spirit right then. Later, the twelfth person of the Edgar Cayce group turned his life over to the Lord and was filled with the Holy Spirit at one of our prayer and praise meetings. Several months later he became a church pastor, beginning a large and effective ministry.

Many times I have looked back at that special time, thanking the Lord for being so faithful, for being willing to work His will through ordinary people.

A Crash Course in Deliverance

Jan and I heard that Don Basham was going to be teaching about deliverance in Avon Lake, about an hour from our home. Don Basham was a very popular teacher in those days and the author of several books. Although it sounded weird, we decided to go and hear what it was all about. Basham was a very laid-back kind of person, the kind whom I like. His teaching was good, all about who Jesus is and how the devil invades our lives at times. Then his message concluded with these words:

"In a short while, I am going to begin teaching about deliverance. Those of you who are not here for that reason should leave now." Many people made their exit, leaving about a hundred in the room. Jan and I stayed. I wasn't there for the deliverance but to learn about it.

Basham removed his jacket, rolled up his sleeves and looked as though he was ready for some contest. I noticed that there were people at the sides of the room with buckets and rolls of paper towels. We weren't ready for what happened next.

"In a moment, I am going to take authority over all evil spirits here in this room. When I do, some of you will need ministry. That is what those people standing are for. They have experience in this sort of thing." During the pause I wondered to myself what was going to happen. "In the name of Jesus Christ, I take authority over the evil spirits in this room."

The room suddenly erupted in pandemonium! Some people began to shriek, others started to shake and jerk, and some fell to the floor. Those who were standing began to move from person to person, taking authority in Jesus' name over the demons that were manifesting themselves. As the leaders did this, the people began to cough and retch. The interesting thing is that they did not vomit food but rather smelly mucous. The people became joyful and calm as the demons left them. I am sure that my eyes were as big as saucers; I was seeing a part of the authority that the name of Jesus has. A couple of children who were there, upon seeing the power of the name, stood up and got into the act, commanding demons to depart. Jan and I didn't say much to each other on the way home that night. I think that we were in an information overload.

God Sends a Woman in Need of Deliverance

The next morning our doorbell rang.

"Hi, Toni (not her real name), what brings you here?"

"I need some help. There are things happening to me over which I have no control. It's as though there is something inside me, making me do things."

Now, I knew why God sent us up to hear Don Basham. Had we not gone to hear him, we wouldn't have known what to do.

"Last night, Toni, Jan and I went to hear a man talk about the deliverance ministry. We learned that sometimes people have an invasion of evil spirits. We know from our experience that in the name of Jesus these evil spirits can be driven out of people so that they are free. If you would like, we will participate in that ministry with you."

Toni did not hesitate. We didn't have to do much preparation because she was surrendered to Jesus and filled with the Holy Spirit. Because I learned at the Basham gathering that demons look at you right through people's eyes, I looked at Toni and said, "In the name of Jesus, I take authority over any evil spirits in Toni. I command you, in the name of Jesus to come out of her."

Suddenly Toni's back arched stiffly. She was in pain. The demon inside her was actually causing physical pain. When we persisted, the pain stayed; when we let up, so did the pain. We told Toni that we needed her cooperation. She needed to take authority over the demon with us.

"I take authority over you, demon, in Jesus' name, and I command you to leave me now."

Then there was coughing and retching followed by a sudden calm. Jan, Toni, and I knew that the demon had gone. Toni went home relieved.

Christians Can Have Demons

In the days to come, I began to gain more experience and understanding about demons. One thing I learned was that Christians can have demons. I had previously heard others teach that it was impossible for a demon to reside in the same body where the Holy Spirit was. If that were the case, then we did deliverance with scores of Christians whom these evangelicals would have termed non-Christians. As I said to one leader, "Then tell me, what do you do when a Christian comes to you in obvious need of deliverance? Do you conclude that the person isn't a Christian?"

I believe demons enter us before we know Christ. Then, we are living with defective or dead spirits. We are totally involved with the world, the flesh, and the devil. God's Spirit doesn't seem to get through our spirits and into our souls. It's as if there is a thick veil keeping God's life from flowing into us. Isaiah was sent to people who experienced such defective spirits. ". . . Go and tell this people: 'Be ever hearing, but never understanding; be ever seeing, but never perceiving.' Make the heart of this people calloused; make their ears dull and close their eyes. Otherwise they might see with their eyes, hear with their ears, understand with their hearts, and turn and be healed" [Isa. 6:9–10].

The minds, emotions, and wills of people without God are totally influenced by the power of the world, the flesh, and the devil. When the soul is unguarded, without God's life and protection, demons may enter and take up residence. The evil spirits' work is to make sure that our hearts are hardened to the things of God. Jesus said, "When anyone hears the message about the kingdom and does not understand it, the evil one comes and snatches away what was sown in his heart" [Matt. 13:1-9]. Paul saw the problem this way: "And even if our gospel is veiled, it is veiled to those who are perishing. The god of this age has blinded the minds of unbelievers . . ." [2 Cor. 4:3-4].

When people hear the message of the kingdom of God and respond to it, they receive new hearts and new spirits [see Ezek. 36:26-32]. The lines of God's communication are now open to those people. But the demons, if there are any present, don't automatically leave. They have to be told to leave. That's why exorcism was part of the initiation rites of the early church. Usually, deliverance from demons was done before people were baptized.

A fourth century bishop, Cyril of Jerusalem, dealt with deliverance in his catechetical lectures: "Submit yourself to be exorcised with all eagerness. Imagine that you had crude gold, adulterated, mingled with all sorts of other substances, such as brass and tin, iron, and lead. It is the gold that we want to have by itself. There is no way of getting gold purged of foreign substances except by using fire. In just the same way, the soul cannot be purged except by exorcisms. . . . The exorcists, by divine Spirit, excite fear, apply fire to the soul in the body for crucible. The demonic enemy is driven out, and there is left salvation: there is left the hope of eternal life."[1]

When Jesus described to Paul his mission, He said it this way: "I will rescue you from your own people and from the Gentiles. I am sending you to them to open their eyes and turn them from darkness to light, and from the power of Satan to God, so that they may receive forgiveness of sins and a place among those who are sanctified by faith in me" [Acts 26:17-18]. *And turn them . . . from the power of Satan to God.* It is obvious that when the new age of God's kingdom came with Jesus, Satan's kingdom was to be destroyed. "He too shared in their humanity so that by his death he might destroy him who holds the power of death—that is, the devil—and free those who all of their lives were held in slavery by their fear of death" [Heb. 2:14-15]. John said that the reason Jesus came "was to destroy the devil's work" [1 John 3:8].

The joy is this: we already have a victory over the power of the devil. That victory was won through the blood shed on the cross. All we have to do is participate in the benefits of that victory. If we have demons, then we have the power to get rid of them. If we are free of demons, then we have the power to stay free.

Seventy Demons

"Helen, could you come over to my office?" I never liked to counsel people alone, especially women. So I had several women I could call at a moment's notice to come and help me. "I have someone here who needs deliverance." Helen arrived not long after I called.

The woman with whom we were going to do ministry was a well-educated person, a leader in the diocese. Things weren't right in her life. Depression, worry, and circumstances had led her to a psychiatrist. But after months of drugs and therapy, she was no better off. As was often the case, our ministry was the court of last resort. Before Helen arrived, I explained about demons, deliverance, and staying free. The woman was ready.

"In the name of Jesus I take authority over any evil spirits in this room." Almost immediately, the woman's arm began to jerk. I knew we were facing a demon, but I wasn't prepared for what was about to happen.

The woman's eyes got a strange sly look and a voice spoke through her mouth, "My name is duplicity." She began to cough, and out came the demon called "duplicity." For some reason "duplicity" was not in my vocabulary so I got the dictionary out to discover its meaning. "Double-mindedness." I wrote it down on my pad.

"My name is envy." A slightly different voice spoke as the woman's face changed, looking like I picture envy. Then the coughing and the release. I continued to write.

"My name is lust." Now the woman's face looked as though she were the epitome of lust. Then the coughing and the release.

Then came one who named himself arthritis. When this happened, a ball of something, about the size of a tennis ball, rose up the woman's back. Helen had her hand right there. Her eyes widened in amazement as the ball passed under her hand. Then the coughing and the release. The most dramatic one came next. The woman's eyes turned yellowish and beady. Her lips began to curl up like a dog snarling. Then she jumped up holding her fingers like claws.

"My name is violence," the demon shouted. I dropped back, but suddenly came the coughing and the release.

Before we finished, I had written down seventy names that demons gave. Each seemed to cause physical changes; each had a different voice modulation. This same woman is now free, doing great things in the church.

Renewal Returns Deliverance to Its Rightful Place

I know that we shouldn't glory in casting out demons; I also know that casting them out is part of Christian work. It is what the disciples were told to do when they went on their training mission. *Not to cast demons out leaves people in the lurch.* For decades and longer, the church at large has gotten out of the very important deliverance ministry. It is more popular today to see evil in broad terms but not personalized. As I became aware of the reality of demons, I was thoroughly impressed with their power to disrupt Christians' lives, but more impressed with the power of Jesus' name to expel them. In the early days of learning, I wrote the following:

The Lord has given me a great privilege that has not been given to many Christian ministers whom I know about. This is to be able to minister in Jesus' name for the purpose of casting demons (or evil spirits) out of people. It is unusual for an Episcopal priest to say this, for there aren't many who know what this means. It is not something that is taught in seminary. In fact, we are led to believe that demons are really some psychological problem, and that Jesus would have called demons by other names had He known what we know now.

When I first saw someone ministering deliverance, I became aware of the fact that the devil is real; he really exists. Soon, I knew that any Christian who refuses to acknowledge the devil's reality and dominion will be ineffective in his or her Christian work. This person will always be doing battle in the world without knowing who the real enemy is.

What I have seen in the past year and a half has been worth a lifetime of other experiences, and then some. I have seen people instantly relieved of mental depression, addictions, compulsions, phobias, migraine headaches, epilepsy, mental torments, asthma, anxieties, and many other things. But more important has been the freedom that people gained to praise and respond to the Lord.

I have learned that professional people, who do not know how to take authority in Jesus' name, and in the power of the Spirit, may never cure those people who are desperately bothered by demons. They will psychologize and psychologize, do therapy upon therapy, but never get to the heart of many problems.

A woman I know had been bothered by a "black cloud" of depression that seemed to come and go in her life. Following the birth of her first child, she suffered a postpartum psychosis. Her psychiatric treatment was shock treatments and counseling. Although she was able to function adequately from that time on, the depression never went away. When the "black cloud" came, the depression got worse. No matter how she tried to alleviate the power of the depression, it was still there to haunt her.

"There is one thing that we haven't tried," I said to her. "Deliverance."

"I'll try anything," she responded.

I took her to a woman I know who was doing deliverance ministry. Together we took authority over five demons who were contributing to the depression. One of the demons named himself "schizophrenia." After the deliverance, it seemed like the weight of the world had come off the woman. The amazing result was that the depression never returned.

Besides learning that demons bother people and that there is power in Jesus' name to expel them, I learned that most of our problems are not caused by demons. However, during those early days we had a rash of "demon hunters" who seemed to think they could find demons behind every bush. Because of the excesses of the "demon hunters," many people backed away from a very valid and meaningful ministry. There were also those who got upset when public deliverances were done. Personally, I believe that the church needs to demonstrate its power more by doing public deliverance. After all, that's the way that Jesus did it.

Since those early days, more and more Christians have seen the value of the deliverance ministry. And laypeople are less fearful about it. Many Christian psychologists and psychiatrists routinely practice deliverance as part of their therapy. It is my hope that someday every church will deliver people of demons before they are baptized and set them free if they are already baptized. It is part of the work of the healing church.

8

LEARNING TO BE A HEALING CHURCH

The Blind Receive Sight

The finger of God!

The image of the finger of God writing the commandments for Moses intrigued me, but when I read what Jesus said about driving out demons "by the finger of God" [Luke 11:20], I was even more fascinated. While I ruminated about the finger of God, I missed the point of the verse. I missed "then the kingdom of God has come to you." I missed the idea that God continues to be in this world through the power of the Holy Spirit. It is when we see the evidence of God's presence that we know His kingdom is with us. It is His intention, I discovered, to be with His people and allow them to partake of His kingdom right now.

"Why did you allow that girl to tell such a preposterous story?"

Bill wasn't the only one who expressed his displeasure about Lily giving a testimony. It was a wonderful testimony bearing witness about how she received her sight. I couldn't figure out why people got so angry. I thought they would be excited about hearing how a blind woman received her sight. But they were angry! Later, I realized why.

Lily's testimony was one among many in those early days, but because she was blind, it made for a more spectacular story. She, and her mother and some friends, Roman Catholics from Seven Hills, near Cleveland, came to our prayer and praise meeting. Lily, we were told, had a disease that destroyed the retinas of her eyes. It was incurable, irreversible. They came to us because they heard that we prayed for those in need. They didn't know that we were novices in the healing ministry. We hardly knew how to pray. It's wonderful how God puts such meetings together; none of us knew what was going to happen.

Lily was led to our prayer chair by her mother.

"What would you like to pray for?" I asked.

"I would like to pray that I could see," she replied.

My heart sank. I didn't have faith for something big such as blindness. I'm not sure that I even believed God *could* heal someone who was blind. I was too new in my conversion. But since I was a leader, I didn't want to appear as if I were unsure; I kept a straight face.

"Okay everyone, gather round and place your hands on Lily. Those who feel led to pray should do so."

People gathered around her, placing their hands on her head and shoulders. We were all trying to be faithful to God as prayers were spoken. And when we were finished, nothing had changed. Lily was the same as when she sat down; she still couldn't see. That's exactly what I expected. During the coming week, I didn't think anything more about Lily.

When the next prayer and praise meeting rolled around, there was Lily with her mother and friends.

"I can tell that something is happening," she said. "I am able to see light and dark; sometimes I see things moving."

I was really skeptical now. It was wishful thinking, I thought. I even told her that she should go see her doctor. We prayed with her again despite my unexpressed doubts.

I was surprised to see Lily again the next week. She said that she went to her doctor, telling him what was happening. Her doctor shared my view, explaining to her that her eye problem was incurable, that she would never see again. "Stay away from those people," he warned. Lily, undaunted, said, "But I can definitely see people, but not clearly." We prayed again.

The next week brought the great news: "I am able to read the blackboard at school." We all rejoiced, for the kingdom of God had come upon us. The finger of God had touched Lily's eyes, giving her sight; His kingdom had come. During that next week, Lily's doctor fitted her with glasses!

When Lily shared this on a Sunday morning with our congregation, it was no wonder that some people were angry. First of all, if she was actually healed, then their understanding of truth came into question; they would have to admit they were wrong about God. Second, if the kingdom of God is right upon them, by the power of her testimony, then their lives would have to change. They might even have to submit to God. The best way to avoid the confrontation with God was to deny that He had healed Lily.

There is an interesting side note about Lily's eyesight. She continued to look as if she were blind, for she never focused her eyes on your face—maybe on your neck, ear, or even behind you. I always had the feeling that she wasn't looking at me. So I asked her the question, "Why is it, Lily, that you claim God touched you, yet your eyes never look like you can see?"

"I never asked God to heal my eyes," Lily gently replied, "I only prayed that He would restore my sight."

The Lame Walk

Getting to the point where I could lead people to pray for healing was a big step for me. You would think that all people who lead congregations would be adept in praying for healing. It wasn't so with me. I needed help, someone to show me and others the way. I heard that John Beckett, the Episcopal layman in Elyria, prayed for healing, so I phoned him and asked him to come to a meeting and show us what to do. John was delighted to come and teach us about healing.

I don't remember anything that John taught that evening. I just know that he taught from Scripture about how God still heals people. That idea alone was exciting enough if it was true; John made the evening even more exciting by his demonstration. He showed us how to have people sit in a chair and to pray for them. Then it happened! It really happened! Someone was healed—and not from a headache that you couldn't prove. This was no psychosomatic thing!

A mother brought her son to the front. He was wearing a very long brace that went from his waist to the bottom of his foot. The bottom of the brace had a spring on it. This kept the boy from putting his full weight on his foot. That in turn protected the ball and socket of his hip, which was never formed right from birth.

"Sit back in the chair," John instructed the boy. Then he held his leg in his hand and prayed that God indeed would heal him. Something happened! The boy's leg moved; we could see it. It wasn't long before he complained that the brace was hurting. I didn't want to take it off, for

I had heard stories about charlatan faith healers telling people to throw their crutches away. So, we loosened the brace with instruction that the mother should take him back to their doctor.

That week the boy returned to the doctor. X-rays were taken and a miracle had taken place. The boy's hip joint was recreated! The only problem was the long disuse of the leg. It was considerably shorter than the other. The doctor gave the mother a prescription for a built-up shoe. The boy was back again the next week for more prayer, his mother determined that God was going to finish the job. God gave me a strong measure of faith this time.

"Let's all gather round and see what God is going to do," I encouraged.

The seventy people present got out of their chairs and moved to where the boy was seated. I had him sit back in the chair, picking up his legs in my hand. It was obvious! One leg was almost an inch and a half shorter than the other.

"Now, let's ask God to heal him."

As we prayed, with the boy's legs in my hands, the short leg began to get longer. We could all see it happening. A young woman behind me sucked in her breath. "I saw it, I saw it!" she exclaimed. Then in the same breath she added, "I did see it, didn't I?"

That's the way with a miracle. It happens so quickly that you can't remember what things were like before it happened.

Some people get nervous when I tell them how God healed this boy and the woman who was blind. I have often gotten the reply, "Well, you know that it is better to seek the healer instead of the healing." These are people who aren't suffering, or who don't have impediments that need healing. It's easy for them to say, "Seek the healer." But healing is important to Jesus. He told the followers of John the Baptist to tell him, "The blind receive sight, the lame walk, those who have leprosy are cured, the deaf hear, the dead are raised, and the good news is preached to the poor" [Luke 7:22]. Yes, we must always be pointing people toward our Lord so that they can have a relationship with Him. But if we are faithful, we will heal the sick too. When we preach Christ, we should expect God to confirm His word with signs, just as Mark described. "Then the disciples went out and preached everywhere, and the Lord worked with them and confirmed his word by the signs that accompanied it" [Mark 16:20]. If "Jesus Christ is the same yesterday and today and forever" [Heb. 13:8], then He is still available to heal people.

Kingdom Living Brings Health Wholeness

George Eldon Ladd, in a wonderful book, *The Gospel of the Kingdom*, speaks of the complexities in understanding the kingdom of God. He describes it, on one hand, as the "realm of the Age to Come," and, on the other, as a kingdom that we may experience in part today. Although the kingdom is here now, he relates, it will come in its perfection.[1] We partake of this kingdom when we become God's children. While we are clothed in our earthly bodies, the substance of our blessing is always in a state of being perfected. When the day of the Lord comes, everything about us will become new and perfect.

What I didn't know was that Christians are supposed to become part of and enjoy the new life that the kingdom of God provides, and so I was not benefiting from what God wanted me to experience. He even gave me His Holy Spirit to lead the way, but I paid not enough attention; and had it not been for the Korvers, whose ministry made me aware of the Holy Spirit, I wouldn't enjoy God's kingdom's blessings that I now enjoy. Because of Jesus, all Christians can not only be restored, forgiven, healed, and changed, but they can enjoy an abundant life as well [see John 10:10].

After John came to help us with healing, I spent more time studying the Scriptures, learning that God is a loving healer. It became very clear that He ardently desires to bless people. All He asks is that they follow the path of blessing He has planned for them. This is what He said to Israel: "I will restore you to health and heal your wounds" [Jer. 30:17]. This promise also belongs to the church. A church that is obedient to God's will is a church that will see the lives of the people changing for the better. They will become healthier physically, emotionally, and mentally; they will begin to live holier lives and exhibit the fruit of the Holy Spirit. As they are clothed with Christ [see Rom. 13:14; Gal. 3:27], they will become more and more whole in this life and better prepared for the life to come.

Expecting Miracles

The gates of healing were opening; and we were beginning to have our expectations increase, believing that God would do wondrous things in our midst. At one time we hung a banner in the church saying "Expect a Miracle." Soon, I began to dream about what would happen as our congregation became more obedient to God. In my mind's eye I saw people praising and worshiping God with great enthusiasm and intensity. The people had open minds and hearts that soaked in the Word of God as they listened to their teachers. The people were spreading the gospel and ministering to the poor. I saw people on their knees, interceding for the work of the church. Others were falling on their knees as they heard the gospel message, joy on their faces as they encountered the risen Christ. I saw people laying hands on others for healing, with those being healed rising up to rejoice. Demons were fleeing as the glory of God descended.

This vision was so different from my previous church experience. The congregations I had been part of were shackled by denominational and local traditions. The people of the world dismissed us as being ineffectual, powerless, and dead. We were on the verge of giving the empty church testimony where the person of Jesus Christ is no longer encountered, where the power and authority of the Holy Spirit are not experienced, and where what little faith there is comes from reason, which is not inspired by the power of God. Thank you, Lord, for rescuing me from such a deadly church environment.

Visitation in the Cobalt Room

Vera was a member of St. Luke's before I arrived. She was a nice lady in her late forties, a traditional Episcopalian with little knowledge of God. I went to the hospital to see her because they were doing tests to pinpoint her cancer. When I asked her if I could pray with her for healing, her response was very positive. However, she wanted to get out of bed and sit next to her new boyfriend before I prayed. As she was getting up, I noticed that her friend's arm was in a sling. I distinctly heard God tell me to pray for him.

"Lord Jesus, I pray to the Father in your name, asking Him to heal Larry of his problem." As I prayed, I put my hand on his shoulder. Instantly Larry was healed of a bursitis condition that had pained him for almost six months! Then I prayed with Vera, but nothing seemed to happen. I did, however, present the gospel to her, emphasizing that she should turn her life over to God. I also told her about being baptized in the Holy Spirit.

After the tests, Vera was supposed to receive cobalt treatments for her cancer. This was her testimony:

"I waited to go into the cobalt room with the rest of the people who were going to have treatments. While I was there, I thought about what you told me about Jesus. Then they wheeled me in, and the treatment began. Just then, Jesus met me in the room. I surrendered my life to Him and was filled with the Holy Spirit. Before I knew it, I was speaking in tongues."

After that meeting with Christ, Vera's symptoms abated and she enjoyed many years of good health before the symptoms returned. I thought about Vera a lot. It wasn't the physical healing that was important to her but the healing that took place in her soul. God gave her a time of good health, but more so, He gave her wholeness in her life. Paul's word about God's "incomparably great power for us who believe" [Eph. 1:19] came true in Vera's life.

The Healing Church

The church, which was empowered in the Upper Room, is still being empowered to this day. The promise is that when we gather in fellowship, we will be able to experience what other disciples have experienced. The Lord was present with them, and people were healed in many different ways. "The apostles performed many miraculous signs and wonders among the people" [Acts 5:12]. These signs and wonders had great effect on the people, both in Jerusalem and surrounding towns. What was happening at St. Luke's was having an effect on those who lived in surrounding communities. The word was spreading that God was with us.

If we visualize the church as a powerful reconciling and healing body, we will not be exceeding the limits of God's redemptive acts. We might, however, exceed the limits of our present experience and expectations. *The healing process is limited only when we fail to embrace all of its possibilities.* If we limit God in any way, then we declare that He is weak. If we say that He has no intention of healing His people, then we declare that healing gifts are not healing gifts after all. "By his wounds you have been healed" [1 Peter 2:24]. The healing that is promised to us is real healing, the same kind that Jesus performed. Jesus not only opened the door for salvation, He opened it for healing and wholeness as well. In fact, salvation and healing go hand in hand.

Every time God met someone to bring healing and wholeness, our faith increased. After a time I began to see a vision for our congregation. We were a healing community. I wrote down and gave to the members what I believed God was doing in our midst:

> We are all bound for the promised land, "the Holy City, the new Jerusalem, coming down out of heaven from God," to dwell with Him forever. It is not how or when we shall get there but rather *who we shall become on the way.* We are the people of God who have been called out of darkness and into God's glorious light, not only so we can be for God's praise but also for His glory. We are called to be a people who demonstrate the power of God's kingdom in this world by doing what Jesus did and even greater works than those.

> Directly ahead of us are the "powers of this dark world" and the "forces of evil in the heavenly realms." We are facing the devil who will use his multiple schemes to trick us into taking our eyes off of Jesus and putting them on the distractions of old life, of darkness. He will divide us when we tolerate only our own purity, so as to pull up the tares. The devil's schemes will be defeated as we grow in our Lord Jesus, demonstrating the depth of our love for one another and our willingness to travel to the promised land together.

> The church's special calling is to take as many others into the promised land as possible by obeying the Great Commission. We, as the church, are called to be a healing community which will help each Christian live into the potential of his or her new life. *A healing community is a body of believers that is in constant community with our Lord Jesus, through the Holy Spirit, and with the people He is saving, sanctifying, and healing.* It concentrates on communicating hope to the discouraged and distraught, deliverance to the oppressed and tormented, forgiveness to the guilt ridden, salvation to the godless, healing to the diseased and maimed, and love to the unlovable. A healing community commits itself to be naturally supernatural. It celebrates its common life through a liturgy of praise and worship for God the Father, God the Son, and God the Holy Spirit.

Then I offered a plan whereby our congregation could become a healing community. It began by developing our common life and by putting the work of ministry in laypeople's hands.

Unwrapping the Grave Clothes

When a person reads "if anyone is in Christ, he is a new creation; the old has gone, the new has come!" [2 Cor. 5:17], it sounds as if everything is finished, that we have all the new life we are supposed to experience. Some people believe that they are instantly sanctified. I knew that wasn't true because none of the people I knew were perfect. We were all in some stage of growing in Christ. This growth process is called sanctification. We are in the process of having our old lives decrease while our new ones increase. John the Baptist said, "He must become greater and greater, and I must become less and less" [John 3:30 TLB]. I like to describe sanctification as salvation's process. Paul spoke of it this way, "You were taught, with regard to your former way of life, to put off your old self, which is being corrupted by its deceitful desires; to be made new in the attitude of your minds; and to put on the new self, created to be like God in true righteousness and holiness" [Eph. 4:22–24].

The process of salvation is similar to Lazarus' experience when he was dead and already decaying in the tomb. When Jesus walked into the tomb and spoke to the dead man, the Holy Spirit immediately gave him life. The life-giving process, however, was not over. As John reports, "The dead man came out, his hands and feet wrapped with strips of linen, and a cloth around his face. Jesus said to them, 'Take off the grave clothes and let him go'" [John 11:44]. That's what a healing community is all about. Christ gives new life to people, but the church helps remove the grave clothes so that a person can be free.

As we are redeemed from the bondage of sin, Satan, and death, the process of our salvation begins [see Acts 26:16–18; 1 John 3:8; Col. 1:13–14]. Although we enter God's family as individuals, salvation's process, or sanctification, is a church family matter. The body of Christ is given the full presence of the Holy Spirit "who is given as a pledge of our inheritance, with a view to the redemption of God's own possession . . ." [Eph. 1:14 NASB]. This guarantees two things: the fullness of our life in God's family, and the assurance of what is to come. Our sins are justified, or forgiven, as God accepts us, and personal development starts through sanctification. When the Day of the Lord comes and Jesus returns, the process will be completed and salvation fully realized. This means that there is a lot of work for the church to do until our Lord returns.

It is God's will that each Christian be totally free from the disease of life with which the kingdom of darkness afflicted us. Through the church we receive all the godly help that we need until all the effects of disease are removed. It is a mistake to see sanctification as an individual concern only. Someone might say it this way: "I was saved on January 14, 1975, and now I am sinless and holy." This, then, becomes the justification for not growing in Christ or participating in fellowship. This person sees no need for the church and the power of God manifested through it. We had one man in St. Luke's who carried this to extremes. At a certain point he considered that his personal sanctification was complete and that allowed him to become the judge of the others in whom it was not complete. I was never able to convince him otherwise. He was missing out on the gifts and ministries that God was providing through the church.

Augustine spoke of our new life in Christ this way: "They came old into the Baptistry and went out new—came in aged and went out infants. Their old life was somnolent age: their new life is the infancy of regeneration . . . After the forgiving and wiping away of all sins, our life amidst the temptations of this world may not avoid all stain . . . [God] is faithful and just to forgive us our transgressions [should we fail]: but only if you are never self-satisfied, if you are *always being made perfect through change.*"[2] Peter says, "Like newborn babies, crave pure spiritual milk, so that by it you may grow up in your salvation" [1 Peter 2:2].

Paul speaks about the continuous process of sanctification or healing by reminding us, "Continue to work out your salvation with fear and trembling, for it is God who works in you to will and to act according to his good purpose" [Phil. 2:12–13]. This is a corporate process, one in which the entire church must be engaged. An Anglican scholar once wrote that we "are not redeemed as separate individuals: we are one body, of which Christ is the Head."[3]

The more I saw God at work healing people, the more I became convinced that every congregation is called to be a healing community. The church is the present fulfillment of Jesus' words, ". . . I have come that they may have life, and have it to the full" [John 10:10]. Our lives are so complex that healing becomes very complex. It is no wonder that only the Holy Spirit can make sense out of any of it. If our church is devoted to being all that God expects of us, then we must be ready to learn more and more about how God can touch the complexities of our lives with ministries and gifts. Pastor John Wimber saw that there are six different interrelated levels of healing that must be practiced in every church:

1. Healing of the spirit (spiritual sickness caused mainly by sin).
2. Healing of past hurts (memories and emotions).
3. Healing of the body (organic and functional problems).
4. Healing of the demonized (often seen as psychic or mental illness).
5. Healing of relationships (the social aspect of people).
6. Healing of the dying and the dead (comforting and strengthening the dying, and raising—not resurrecting—the dead.[4]

When a congregation is at its best, it will be using the gifts of the Spirit and the authority and power which Jesus provides to heal the people within the body. When this healing begins to take place, it will be so compelling that when others see it they will be drawn to our Lord. Since we are to be a people who are naturally supernatural, this should pose no problem. It is obvious to me that a healing church will be a community of people who love as Christ loves.

Healing Steps

I was learning about God and healing, step by step. As I took each step, I shared with the congregation my insights. This point was the most important: I learned that *the first step toward healing is a relationship with Jesus Christ.* Without Jesus there is no salvation and no healing. It was said of the shepherds of the Jewish "church" that they sinned against God by neglecting to strengthen the weak, heal the sick, and bind up the injured [see Ezek. 34:4]. The Good Shepherd, however, whom we know to be Jesus, restores to the church what it lost through poor leadership. It is Jesus, the incarnate God, who now enters into personal relationships with all whom He strengthens, heals, and binds up. The ministry of Jesus now becomes the ministry of the church. We first help people to come into a relationship with Jesus, and then He empowers us to become part of their sanctification, their healing process.

The second step toward healing is to be incorporated into God's family. The spiritual gifts that God gives for our healing and growth are received when we are part of Christian fellowship. When our congregation was small, it was easy for us to have fellowship as an entire group. But as we grew, it became more apparent that people needed smaller groups in which to find their healing and growth. We began to learn about the value of small cell groups of people who meet together on a regular basis. Cells reach out to include others in God's kingdom and they bless one another so that healing and growth take place. It is in these relationships that the brokenness of a person's life can be lovingly and powerfully touched again and again.

The third step toward healing is the strengthening of our natural family. Life with Christ means that He will bring holy order into our natural family life. It leads toward the day when both husband and wife agree with Joshua, each saying, "But as for me and my household, we will serve the LORD" [Josh. 24:15]. The more marriage becomes an expression of "one body," the more the power of God will be there to bring healing. "The family," according to Cardinal Suenens, "provides the primary experience of Christian community . . . It is also the starting point for all other community life."[5]

The fourth step toward healing is worship with the larger community. Praising God, praying for one another, hearing God's Word preached, receiving holy Communion, and hearing testimonies of God's action in our lives is essential to our soul's health. Sunday is the time when the small cell groups gather together for celebration. It is often in the midst of praise and worship that we experience God's strong presence. At such a time people may be healed and delivered from evil spirits.

My own attitude about what a healing community meant was changed again and again. One of the first things that I inaugurated on Sunday morning was healing prayers following the service. Those who had needs were invited to remain for prayer. I offered these prayers after the main service because I didn't want to offend the old-timers who didn't believe in healing. It wasn't long, however, before I realized that healing gifts needed to be part of our life together, not something to be shunted off to the corner. As a result, I began to increase teaching about healing. Then I included prayers for healing during the Sunday morning service. The time that seemed best was following holy Communion. As people received Communion, they could then walk over to the prayer team which was ready to pray with them. The response was tremendous. Many people came for prayer every Sunday, revealing the great need in every congregation for people to be healed and strengthened.

Real Live Stuff

Sanctification, salvation's process, is real life stuff. As we are being made perfect or whole in Christ it involves our real flesh and blood lives. It is the time when the divine becomes increasingly incarnate in us. So the promise of salvation not only means that we will be acceptable in heavenly places, but it means that there will be a heavenly infusion in our present lives.

The Greek word for salvation, *soteria,* can be translated as "health." It implies much more than a future life to come. Instead it speaks of the direct involvement of the Holy Spirit in our lives. It must involve the entire person, lest we fall into the old Gnostic heresy of dualism. Dualism would have us believe that all created things are part of an evil realm while the spiritual is separate and good. This heresy is expressed when people are encouraged to become more "spiritual," and thus more removed from the world. They can call the world "evil" and remove themselves or defend themselves from it. They take on a "fortress" mentality.

God was incarnate in Jesus' real physical body. The Holy Spirit's work of causing us to be born again is done in our physical bodies. The reassurance of God's presence is placed in earthen vessels [see 2 Cor. 4:7]. God's purpose is not to make us less and less earthen, but to bring all that is earthen into submission to Him, controlled by the Spirit. It is God's intention that we become as perfectly human as was Jesus until we receive our promised imperishable body at the Lord's Day [see 1 Cor. 15:35–58].

Salvation's promise always looks forward to its fulfillment. This, however, is not "pie in the sky" but bread on the table. It is the perfect understanding of what was meant when God said, "Man does not live on bread alone, but on every word that comes from the mouth of God" [Deut. 8:3]. The perfecting or sanctification of God's people begins with the Holy Spirit, who applies God's word in our lives, making all things new. As people become captive to Christ, He makes supernatural provision so that people are sanctified. This involves the whole person—one's character, personality, thought process, relationships, work, and estate.

When the wholeness of sanctification is seen in its narrowest sense, people do not receive the blessings that are part of a full Christian life. After being set free from the effects of sin and death, people must walk in this freedom, this new life. The whole person is involved in this walk. This caused John to say that if a person continued in sin after being rescued from it, then he was still being ruled by the devil. "If we claim to have fellowship with him yet walk in the darkness, we lie and do not live by the truth" [1 John 1:6].

Healing happens when God's people become what He intends them to be [see Eph. 2:22] and do what He intends them to do [see Eph. 2:10]. These are the two main thrusts of gospel life, becoming and doing. You can't have one without the other. When one becomes more like Christ, she is being restored from the effects of the disease of darkness; thus she receives healing. Then when a person does the work of Christ, he brings salvation and its healing to others. When that person continues to disciple those who have come into salvation, then the grave clothes are unwrapped and sanctification or healing continues.

When people understand the full message of salvation, they will be more apt to be delivered from the disease of the old life by appropriating the new. It is up to the church to make every possible provision for the continued growth of its people in Christ. Sanctification or healing cannot be limited to character development or to a few people with healing gifts. When the church community utilizes all of the gifts that God is providing for the edification and building up of his people, then the church family will become healthy. God gives the church strengthening gifts of the Spirit to speed this process of making people whole. The bumper sticker which says, "Be patient, God isn't through with me yet," is an apt statement. Whatever God isn't through with yet isn't healed, but by God's grace it can be.

Perfect in Christ

It has always been God's purpose that the church be made whole in Christ, so that it could be a perfect bride: "to present her to himself as a radiant church, without stain or wrinkle or any other blemish, but holy and blameless" [Eph. 5:27]. The rise of individual religion has so narrowed the horizons concerning the maturing of the church that much of salvation's healing process has been overlooked. The church has always been in the healing business from the day that Christ went about making people well. He not only healed, He forgave their sins. His ultimate concern was to see people reconciled to God. But this reconciliation had to involve more than a person's soul.

As the truth of God's life is brought to bear upon the lives of God's people, they are being restored to wholeness. One church father, Irenaeus, asked the following: "How, then, are the sick to be made strong? And how are sinners to repent? Is it by persevering as they are? Or, on the contrary, by undergoing a great change and reversal of their previous behavior by which they brought upon themselves serious illness and many sins? Ignorance, the mother of these things, is driven out by knowing the truth."[6]

If the local church body is functioning in the manner in which it could, then its members would be changed by "attaining to the whole measure of the fullness of Christ" [Eph. 4:13]. A literal rendering of this passage might say, "become complete according to the stature of the fullness of Christ." In other words, we get so full of Christ that there is no more old life to be seen. That change will prove that it is God who is at work in our mortal bodies [see 2 Cor. 4:7].

The Reverend George Stockhowe once talked about a well that was full of water, as we might say that we were full of Christ. He showed that the well could actually hold more water if the debris inside it were removed. He said that the same is true of our lives. We may claim to be full of Christ, but as long as there is the debris of old life within, then we really aren't as full as we could be. This is the work of the healing church—removing the old life so that we can be full of God.

9

FACING OPPOSITION

Intimidation

"Where is Bob? I haven't seen him for quite awhile." The vestryman (church board member) looked directly at me when he asked it. Inwardly, I experienced disapproval. The reason he said that, I thought, was to imply that the change of direction at St. Luke's had driven Bob away. Being intimidated by his question, I began to offer excuses. I never like to have anyone criticize me. The weight of one critical statement was like a ton while positive statements weighed ounces. One harsh statement could take the wind out of my sails.

What I really wanted to say in response to the vestryman's question was, *You know as well as I that Bob is a good Christmas and Easter churchman. Why are you using him as a way of hiding your true feelings? You are the one who is upset with the way things are. Others in the church cover up their feelings and say things like, "Everyone is concerned." Again you know as well as I that Bob was never a good member of this church, even before I came.* However, I didn't respond in this manner. I only reacted as if I had been stepped on by an elephant.

Much of the criticism that came my way was poorly informed and usually created from hearsay evidence. One woman in the congregation had written me off quickly when I gave testimony to how God changed my life despite the fact that Jan and I spent considerable time in her home. We mistakenly thought we were friends.

"I'm bothered by the things that you are doing on those nights [speaking of prayer and praise meetings]. I understand that you are having seances." This comment really hurt. There is nothing more abhorrent to one who loves the Lord than a seance. Anything connected with the occult is forbidden territory. We had already learned that the devil's things, such as fortune telling, palm reading, astrology, and the like were to be renounced.

No matter how difficult it is to be effective while being criticized, there is something on the inside that makes me feel I must press on with the work before me. God's entrance into my life was not only fulfilling but also satisfying. I was now in the process of learning that as a child of God, I must be obedient to Him. I had much to learn in this area.

Failing the Big Test

My first great testing since being baptized in the Holy Spirit happened on Pentecost Sunday that first year. I was preaching at the eight o'clock service:

"I know and can attest to the fact that the gifts of the Holy Spirit still belong to the church. What happened at Pentecost still happens today. I can give testimony to this reality."

As I was preaching, a man, sitting in the middle of the congregation, gave a loud sneering laugh. I was so startled that I lost my train of thought. I stared at him for a few seconds in disbelief. This was a highly respected man, not the type to do such a thing. I waited until the service was over and rushed to get to the door before the man was able to leave the church.

"Why did you do that?"

"I've heard what is going on at the ten o'clock service."

"What do you mean, going on?" I was already irritated.

"I've heard all about what you are doing, speaking in tongues and all. It isn't scriptural!" With that, the man brushed past me and headed for his car. I was right after him with my nose in his face.

"Look," I blurted out, my anger showing, "I don't understand how you, the chairman of the board of a large multi-national corporation, can accept secondhand information without checking it out. No one is speaking in tongues at that service. There's nothing different about it. You are wrong!"

He got into his car and sped away, never to return to St. Luke's. I knew that he was wrong, so I felt justified. That feeling only lasted for awhile; I soon discovered that there was no adequate justification for my anger and the way I expressed it. Later, I apologized to him. But no matter how he felt about me and what I was doing, there was no way that I could back away from God's appointed work.

I learned later why this man was so upset. He was from an evangelical background; he had supported the efforts of people such as Billy Graham, and he was a fine Christian man. Many evangelicals and most fundamentalists make a scriptural error. They assume, without good biblical support, that we are in a new dispensation. Now that we have the Bible, they insist, there is no need for gifts of the Spirit. So, they say supernatural things ended in the first century or shortly thereafter. It is difficult for a person steeped in dispensationalism to understand a God who is pouring out his Holy Spirit in this day.

The Leaders Put to the Test

At our next vestry meeting, a representative of the man in question appeared. This was the man, I learned, who was supplying the erroneous information. But we didn't know that fact when he addressed our leaders: "I have been instructed by 'the man' to tell you that either Chuck Irish leaves this parish or he will go with his money." I could hardly believe what I was hearing. Even then, I doubted that this person could have been sent by "the man." I was sure that he had done it on his own. Nevertheless, this was powerful! "The man" in question was the "cash box" of the parish. He had always bailed it out when it fell behind or took on major projects. He was even responsible for the rebuilding of the rectory in which Jan and I were living.

The representative's manner was rather pompous and abrasive, causing the leaders to react against him. "We are sorry that he has to leave," was their decision, speaking almost as one. I breathed a sigh of relief and thanked the Lord; I had never expected it to turn out that way. Had the man been a little smoother, the reaction might have been different. Surely I was learning the lesson that when a man obeys God, God blesses the work. And I was confident that I was obeying God.

Taking a Spiritual Inventory

That evening I knew that I had to find out the spiritual health of the parish, to find out each person's relationship with the Lord and whether or not they were baptized in the Holy Spirit. I began with the vestry, for if these leaders were not surrendered to the Lord, then they wouldn't support what God wanted us to be and do. When I assessed the spiritual health of the vestry, I found that the majority were either converted to God or their spouses were. I began to feel a bit more confident. After this, I began to take a spiritual inventory of the entire congregation. So that I was not judgmental, I asked each person about his or her relationship with God so that each could answer for himself.

The Bishop Speaks for God

However, my confidence was shattered within a few days. "I don't know how to tell you this," Bill said almost apologetically, "but I've heard that Mr. Jones (not his real name, the same man that I had confronted) is getting all of the charter members of our congregation together. He is going to wait for you to go on vacation and then have a meeting to get you out." Such a threat was not to be taken lightly, for the congregation had been successful in getting my predecessor out of the parish. The head layman (senior warden) had been elected on the platform that he could get him out.

This was the first time that Jan and I had planned to take an entire month for vacation. We could never afford a vacation before. This time we had found a place in Canada, and we could afford to go. And now this! I was so discouraged, thinking that my time at St. Luke's was coming to an end. They were going to get me when I was defenseless. I wouldn't have known what to do even had I stayed around.

Bishop Burt was on vacation, but I thought that this was important enough for me to call him. Because St. Luke's was a mission, the bishop had jurisdiction over my future there. After some difficulty convincing his secretary of the importance of the call, I was given the number.

"Bishop Burt, this is Chuck Irish. I hate to bother you while you are on vacation, but something rather important has come up, and I thought that I had better let you in on it." I had always found Bishop Burt ready to talk with anyone who had a problem. There was no hesitation in his response to me.

"Tell me what the problem is."

I did the best I could to describe what had been told to me—that Mr. Jones, the "purse strings" of the congregation, was disgruntled and now organizing a move to get rid of me while I was on vacation. (Later I discovered that some people had already discussed my future with the Bishop.)

I continued. "I don't want to be the cause for a division in the congregation. I will be glad to resign now if you think I should." The Bishop's response startled me.

"You started something. Finish it."

"But Bishop," I pleaded, "remember who this man is. I don't want to cause you to lose out on any gifts from his family." (His family had recently given several million dollars to the Episcopal Church.)

"You started something. Finish it!" I didn't know it then, but I did later: God had spoken to me through Bishop Burt. God had not rescued me from disillusionment and despair and set me on a path where I was being guided by his Holy Spirit only to have me give up at the first sign of trouble.

The Holy Spirit Confronts People with Christ

Later, I heard of clergy who quit their renewal efforts at the first signs of trouble. They worried that somehow the Holy Spirit would lead them into something divisive, as if God could be wrong. Yet, I was learning that one of the works of the Holy Spirit is to confront people with Jesus Christ. "When he comes, he will convict the world of guilt in regard to sin and righteousness and judgment: in regard to sin, because men do not believe in me" [John 16:8–9]. It is like a pruning process. When light comes into the darkness, the darkness sometimes stands in opposition. Some people, as a result of God's confrontation, will choose to oppose Him and everyone who represents Him. This kind of divisiveness is Holy Spirit divisiveness, and it is good.

I have thanked God for Bishop Burt many times since that telephone call. I have always found him to be supportive, even if we disagreed about something. That one incident was a milestone for me. It was something I remembered when I had trouble and was tempted to be discouraged. I could hear God saying to me, "I started something through you. Let me finish it."

10

A SANITY CHECK

A Visitor from England Storms Out

I tried my best to be friends with all those who thought of me as their enemy. Although Mr. Purse Strings had chosen to oppose me, I made every effort to make him a friend. Since that time I have often wondered what would have happened if I hadn't gotten angry and blown up in the beginning. I have known since that time that "the man" really didn't understand anything of what was happening.

In order to check things out, I was told, he had breakfast with Billy Graham in an effort to find out more about charismatic renewal. From what I could tell, the meeting didn't produce his hoped-for results. But in those days many leaders were concerned about charismatic renewal. The church had only talked about the Holy Spirit; few had experienced the supernatural outpouring of Pentecost.

"The man," however, hadn't exhausted all of his resources to get to the bottom of the matter. My guess is that he thought I was a bit shy of a full brain. He wasn't the only one. A lot of people thought that after a time I would "come to my senses." I know that even my own father was sure (till he was converted) that I had gone off the deep end. What "the man" did was have his nephew from England come to my home to examine me.

The nephew was a young man and very bright. One Sunday he showed up in church and introduced himself. He told me that he wanted to talk with me about what was going on. He probably wondered if he was on a wild goose chase because our Sunday church service was very ordinary—except for the enthusiasm of the people. I invited him to come for lunch.

"My uncle is concerned with what is happening in the church these days. Since I just came over, could you tell me what is happening?"

By this time I was always ready to give my testimony to others. Here was someone who was asking for it. I drew up my chair, looked him in the eye, and began the story. I told him how I had been so disillusioned because I didn't see the power of God at work, that I had made the decision to leave the ministry, and then I had the encounter with the Korvers. I told him about the baptism in the Holy Spirit and how not only was my life changed, but that scores of other members were changed also. He listened intently as I continued, but I could tell that he was getting a bit nervous.

"Since that time, many wonderful things have happened in our congregation. There have even been miracles. Why, there was even a blind girl who had her sight restored at one of our prayer and praise meetings."

I hardly had the words out of my mouth when the young man literally jumped out of his chair and shouted at me.

"How presumptuous can you be!"

With that he left the house, never to return. He and his uncle must have had a very interesting conversation on his arrival home. But in those days it was not unusual to think that a person sold out to Jesus Christ was a bit unbalanced. Later, I met a doctor whose wife had him committed to a mental institution because he was baptized in the Holy Spirit and spoke in tongues. She was later converted. It still happens today. *USA Today* reported on June 17, 1992, about a young man who was wrongly diagnosed as a paranoid schizophrenic because he spoke in tongues.

11

BACK TO THE UPPER ROOM

Three Catholic Priests Filled with the Holy Spirit

I was proud of my "Jesus the Great Garbage Collector" sermon. I had made all of the possible symbolism work for me.

As I looked out over the people who filled our small church, I was convinced that many would respond to my word. I was ready to make the invitation.

"If you would like to surrender your life to Jesus and be baptized in the Holy Spirit, please come forward now."

Almost immediately three men got up from the back pew and rushed forward. I was more proud of myself than ever as each was filled with the Holy Spirit and began to speak in tongues.

Later, I had a conversation with the three men. They happened to be Byzantine Catholic priests who were disillusioned with their ministry and were on leave as they tried to make decisions for the future. Someone had told them about what was happening at St. Luke's. They came because they really wanted to serve the Lord, thinking that this might be the answer.

"We could hardly wait for you to finish talking and get on with the praying. We had already decided before we came that we were going to pray for the baptism in the Holy Spirit." My ego was smashed.

Each priest, when filled with the Holy Spirit, was supernaturally given a new perspective on ministry. No longer were they disillusioned, wondering if God was at work. One became a lay-worker in the church, one brought renewal to several parishes, and the third became the president of a seminary.

Hebrew—A Language of the Spirit

One of these priests, Father Seraphim, brought a young man to me who was very troubled. In the early days of my ministry, I would have judged this man a candidate for a mental hospital. However, I knew now that he needed the help only God could give. It took quite a while for the Lord to break through into his life, but break through He did. There came a time when it seemed right that we should pray for Joe to receive the baptism in the Holy Spirit. He needed power from God to do what he needed to do. (Today that young man is an Episcopal priest.)

"Remember, Joe, Jesus is the baptizer in the Holy Spirit. Just ask Him to do it and He will. He has promised to give more of the Holy Spirit to those who will ask Him." Father Seraphim was kneeling beside Joe.

"Jesus, I pray that you will baptize me in the Holy Spirit." Jesus did, and soon Joe began to speak in tongues. As he did, Father Seraphim began to weep. Finally, I went over to him and asked what was wrong.

"It's so beautiful," he said.

"What's beautiful?"

"Joe—he's praising God and glorifying the Trinity in Hebrew." Father Seraphim was a Hebrew scholar. Joe did not know Hebrew.

There was another time when I was praying with people at the altar rail. As I laid my hands on them, I prayed in the Spirit quietly. A woman who was kneeling at the rail jerked her head up in amazement.

"Do you know what you are saying? You are speaking Japanese!" Languages were her forte, Japanese being one of them.

Paul indicated the possibility of speaking both in the tongues of men and angels [see 1 Cor. 13:1]. There are over three thousand languages and dialects in the world today, with many learned but by a few. Beyond these earthly languages, who knows how many heavenly languages are possible for us to speak when we are baptized in the Holy Spirit? One thing is certain: speaking in tongues is made possible by the Holy Spirit. "For anyone who speaks in a tongue does not speak to men but to God . . . he utters mysteries with his spirit" [1 Cor. 14:2].

It is comforting to know that God did not give the languages of the Spirit to His disciples so that they could babble incoherently. This was the suggestion of one source I read: people worked themselves into an emotional frenzy and babble. They called that babbling "glossolalia." Scripture lets us know that speaking in tongues is not babbling. "All of them were filled with the Holy Spirit and began to speak in other tongues *as the Spirit enabled them*" [Acts 2:4, italics mine].

The Power of Praying in the Spirit

Why in the world did God make it possible to speak in tongues? Paul explains simply, "He who speaks in a tongue edifies [builds up] himself" [1 Cor. 14:4]. How wonderful! God has given the church languages, enabled by the Holy Spirit, so that a person can speak mysteries to God and build herself up. No wonder Paul wished that all people spoke in tongues. He even saw it as part of the armor of God. "And pray in the Spirit on all occasions" [Eph. 6:18]. Jude was even more emphatic about speaking in tongues. "But you, dear friends, build yourselves up in your most holy faith and pray in the Holy Spirit" [Jude 20].

"What's all this stress on tongues?" a clergyman once taunted me. "After all it's the least of the spiritual gifts."

"Well," I replied, "if there are gifts which are better than others, which I doubt, then wouldn't it be best if you began with the least? It would be like waiting to be asked to a higher table by the Lord. You wouldn't demand to sit at the Lord's right hand because you didn't want to start at the least, would you?" He didn't have an answer.

"Don't tongues demand an interpretation?" The asker had obviously read the Scripture.

"What you may have failed to recognize," I pointed out, "is that 1 Corinthians 14 identifies two kinds of speaking in tongues. The first is something that is private, edifying the individual, the second is public, edifying the church. The latter demands the interpretation. The private tongue enables the person to carry on a conversation spirit to Spirit. Paul mentioned what he did privately by saying, 'I thank God that I speak in tongues more than all of you'" [1 Cor. 14:18].

For the life of me I cannot figure out why some people are so afraid of speaking in tongues. A person is never out of control, and the benefits are so great. One thing is for sure: If you have never spoken in tongues, then you don't know what it is all about. When a person is baptized in the Holy Spirit, he or she gets the whole package. One thing received is the ability to speak in tongues. All the person has to do is open his mouth and begin to speak. It's a faith matter like Peter getting out of the boat and walking on water. He didn't know that he had the ability to walk on water until he began to do it. One doesn't know that tongues are possible until he begins to talk. I just encourage the person not to talk in English. The strangest part of speaking in tongues is that you don't form the words in your mind before you speak; you speak and hear the words that you are saying.

"I want to assure you," I said to a church group, "that speaking in tongues *is not the evidence* of the baptism in the Holy Spirit. I believe what I once heard David DuPlessis* say, 'Tongues is the *consequence* of the baptism in the Holy Spirit.' It is part of the package. The evidence of the baptism in the Holy Spirit is that you are empowered to serve God. Those who are filled with the Spirit have a release of the Spirit in their lives enabling them to utilize the charismatic gifts of the Holy Spirit in their ministries."

"So," many have asked, "why do you stress speaking in tongues?"

"I only stress it once," is my reply. "If you are going to ask Jesus to baptize you in the Holy Spirit, then you need to know that you will be able to speak in tongues. You need to be encouraged so that you don't fall short of getting something that will build you up spiritually. Once the initial ministry is over, you seldom ever hear me talk about it again. That's because you are enjoying the benefits of speaking in tongues."

The Baptism in the Spirit Belongs in the Church

I have never heard a good explanation as to why the church lost its touch with the Holy Spirit. The early church understood the whole matter and so prayed with the newly baptized to receive the baptism in the Holy Spirit. The initiation process had three elements: exorcism from evil spirits, baptism in water, and baptism in the Holy Spirit. Each gospel and the book of Acts refers to both baptisms; the church baptizes in water, and Jesus baptizes in the Holy Spirit [see Matt. 3:11; Mark 1:8; Luke 3:16; John 1:33; Acts 1:5; 11:16].

"But doesn't the Nicene Creed and the Scripture say that there is only one baptism?"

This question seems to be one of the biggest hang-ups about calling the baptism in the Holy Spirit a second baptism. It is true, there is only

---

*David DuPlessis was a pioneer in charismatic renewal. An author and speaker, DuPlessis was known as "Mr. Pentecost."

"one baptism *for the remission of sin.*" The church only performs one baptism. It is carried out by church leaders in water for the remission of sin. This seems to be the point of Paul's word to people in Jerusalem: "And now what are you waiting for? Get up, be baptized and wash your sins away, calling on his name" [Acts 22:16]. There are other benefits of baptism, of course. The person is adopted as a child of God, made a member of Christ's Body, united with Christ, becomes an inheritor of God's kingdom, and the Holy Spirit is active in her life. This is the consequence of baptism in water for all believers.

The baptism in the Holy Spirit, although usually initiated in the confines of the church, is much different. The baptizer, instead of the leaders of the church, is Jesus. Scripture is clear, saying that Jesus is the baptizer in the Holy Spirit. This baptism is not into water, but into the Holy Spirit. This is the "promise of the Father" that Jesus spoke of. "When the Counselor comes, *whom I will send to you* from the Father . . ." [John 15:26, italics mine].

"But if God wants me to be filled with the Holy Spirit, won't he just do it? Why do I have to ask?"

I remember the young woman being very concerned that she would do something wrong. She was brought up a Southern Baptist. Not only did some Baptists have a problem with the present outpouring of the Holy Spirit, but they were concerned that people might tread on the good graces of the Lord if they were too aggressive with their demands. This woman had learned to be passive with God.

"I know you are worried that you might offend God if you are demanding, as you see it. But think about these Scriptures. The first from James, 'You do not have, because you do not ask God' [4:2]. And this from Jesus, 'You may ask me for anything in my name, and I will do it' [John 14:14]. It seems to be a virtue that God wants us to develop; He wants us to be willing to go to Him and ask Him for what we need. Now listen to what Jesus says about the Holy Spirit, 'How much more will your Father in heaven give the Holy Spirit to those who ask him!'" [Luke 11:13].

The Baptism in the Spirit Awakens Gifts

I have a general observation about what happens to those who are baptized in the Holy Spirit. Their experience is generally the same as mine. First, I was awakened, not only to the reality of Jesus but to an inner desire to praise and worship Him. Jesus became preeminent in my life. Second, I had a hunger to read the Scripture, to absorb everything that I could. I believed that what I read was true. Third, I felt that a boldness was quickened in me, a boldness to trust God as I led people to Christ and prayed with them for healing. The gifts of the Spirit were loosed in my life. The baptism in the Holy Spirit brought the *dunamis* (Greek for power) that I needed to serve God. Without it I would have quit the ministry and become a psychotherapist.

I have talked with hundreds of clergy whose experience of doing ministry was similar to mine. They felt impotent to carry on God's work; they were tired and discouraged. Most felt that the church had let them down by sending them to do things that they were not equipped to do. When they were baptized in the Holy Spirit, they were filled with God and inspired and empowered for the work ahead. It was a new beginning, a sure foundation for ministry.

An Outpouring of the Spirit in Pennsylvania

The people in a Pennsylvania church listened intently as I gave my testimony. They understood that my need for the fullness of God was their need also. No one wants to be a failure as a Christian, and the church had not told them how to be successful.

"Now I want to offer each of you the opportunity to give your lives to Jesus and to be filled with the Holy Spirit. I will go over into another room; those of you who hear God speaking to your hearts, follow me over there. A group of us will pray with you so that you receive all that you desire of God."

I prayed for the people before I moved to the room, asking that God would lead those who should come. Then I walked out of the nave of the church to the large room nearby. Chairs had been set up in a circle; about sixty people came in. Four of us formed two teams. After the people were settled, I led them to renounce Satan and the occult. As always, I encouraged them to do this out loud. Then I talked a moment about forgiving everyone for everything; this was followed by an open forgiving of anyone one who had hurt them in the past. Then they confessed their known and unknown sins. Some of the people were in tears by this time.

"Now, ask Jesus to come into your heart and take up residence. Acknowledge that He is your Savior. Give up your life to Him and ask Him to be the Lord of your life." All of the people earnestly followed the instructions. Most had forgotten that other people were in the room with them.

"Remember, now, that Jesus is the baptizer in the Holy Spirit. All you have to do is ask Him. It's just like this: 'Jesus, baptize me in the Holy Spirit.' When you ask Him He will do it. When He does, you will get the whole package. You will receive the ability to speak in the Spirit. You will be able to speak in tongues. No one will be a second-class citizen. Whether you ever speak in tongues or not, it will be your possession." At times like this, I have always been blessed with boldness. I know that Jesus will be there to answer people's prayers.

"After you ask Jesus to baptize you in the Spirit, lift your hands to God and begin to talk. But don't talk anything that you know. Just trust that God will enable you. I will speak in the language He gives me." At this point a lot of people worry that nothing will happen because they don't hear anything in their mind. But I just encourage them to be bold.

"Now, I am going to speak what God gives me, you do the same. Okay. Let's all do it together." My partner and I began to walk the circle, encouraging each person. As we did, each person in his own manner, began to speak in the language the Holy Spirit gave.

The Upper Room Is a Place of Renewal

As more and more people at St. Luke's in Bath surrendered their lives to the Lord and received the baptism in the Holy Spirit, the manifestations of the gifts of the Spirit began to increase. The first thing that we noticed was the physical healing that was taking place. We were all convinced that God was at work through us. What Paul knew was coming true in our lives. "There are different kinds of gifts, but the same Spirit. There are different kinds of service, but the same Lord. There are different kinds of working, but the same God *works all of them in all men*" (italics mine) [1 Cor. 12:4–6]. Now, our church body was being built up through the working of the Holy Spirit. At times I felt like a spectator at some wonderful event.

The Upper Room experience was a place of beginning for St. Luke's parish renewal. It began as my life and ministry were supernaturally changed. As a result of this encounter with God, all that I had hoped for in ministry began to be realized. The bottom line was that *people were being converted and their lives changed*. God was at work. Although my Upper Room wasn't the same as the one in which Jesus poured out the promise of the Father [see Acts 1:4] upon the 120 or so disciples, it is the same Pentecost outpouring of the Holy Spirit that they experienced. It is the same Pentecost reality that Christians have continued to receive from that first day. It is the same Pentecost experience which the family of Cornelius [see Acts 10:44–46] experienced, and of which Peter spoke when he told the disciples, "I remembered what the Lord had said, 'John indeed baptized with water, but you shall be baptized with the Holy Spirit'" [Acts 11:16]. *If we believe Peter, then every believer can experience the same.* "The promise is for you and your children and for all who are far off—for all whom the Lord our God will call" [Acts 2:39]. The essential understanding is this: *The power of Pentecost that made ministry possible for the early disciples is still available to believers today. This filling of the Spirit is not related to salvation, but rather to service.*[1]

The positive purpose of Pentecost is to make ministry possible. *Without Pentecost ministry is impossible.* Jesus knew what he was doing when he ordered the disciples to wait until they got the power they needed [see Luke 24:49]. He knew that they would be unable to fulfill the Great Commission [see Matt. 28:16–20; Luke 24:44–47] without Great Commission power. When the disciples got the power, the results were clear: their emboldened ministry turned the world upside down [see Acts 17:6].

God's Power for the Church

Some renewal begins with the people, some with the clergy; either is able to stop it from happening by quenching the Holy Spirit. When people do quench the Spirit, it usually stems from either fear or ignorance. Fear often arises out of misunderstandings about the working of the Spirit. Sometimes it is because people are afraid of losing control; still another, more important reason is that people fear the truth that will compel them to change their lives. The lack of adequate information produces ignorance and inaccurate preconceptions. Both fear and ignorance combine to deny a person God's provision for life and ministry. The baptism in the Holy Spirit is God's power for ministry. But head knowledge is not enough; *experience* confirms what we know to be true. Often our learned theological hang-ups prevent us from gaining the experience of God that He wishes to give.

I stated earlier that when I was entering the ordained ministry, I had no one to encourage me with spiritual realities. No one told me that I could enter into a personal relationship with Jesus. Later, when I was struggling in the parish, there was no one to tell me that God wanted to fill me with His Spirit so that I could become effective in ministry. I knew that I was called to ordained ministry, but my provision was not sufficient.

It was almost four years after I was ordained that I experienced the reality of being filled with God's life-giving presence and His ministry power, the baptism in the Holy Spirit. My experiential lack was not unique. Thousands of clergy will testify that they experienced God's fullness for ministry many years after their ordination. We should never be too proud to admit when we lack what we need to fulfill our calling to serve God.

R. A. Torrey, seeing that the baptism in the Holy Spirit is part of a disciple's preparation, asks the following: "If the apostles with their . . . exceptional fitting for the work they were to undertake needed this preparation, how much more do we? In light of what Jesus required of his disciples before undertaking the work, does it not seem like the most daring presumption for any of us to undertake to witness and work for Christ until we also have received the promise of the Father, the baptism with the Holy Spirit?"[2]

Torrey asked prospective leaders these questions, "Have you met God?" and "Have you been baptized with the Holy Spirit?" These questions, he said, must be asked of every Christian. "For all Christians are called to ministry of some kind. Any person in Christian work who has not received the baptism in the Holy Spirit ought to stop his work right where he is and not go on with it until he has been 'clothed with power from on high.'"[3]

Could any of us, if we know we have not yet experienced God's empowerment for service, hesitate or refuse to ask Him for such provision? Should you sense that these spiritual realities are lacking in your life, then here are four steps for you to take:

1. If you are able, find someone faithful to God to assist you as you pray. Begin by letting God know that you are seeking Him with all your heart. Tell Him about your life; tell Him what you are lacking. If you do not already experience a personal relationship with Him, then tell Him of your desire. Confess your sins and receive His forgiveness. Forgive all those who have hurt you in any way. Renounce any involvement with the occult, New Age, horoscopes, etc. Renounce the devil and any impact he may have had on your life. Then ask Jesus to

come into your life. Tell Him that you will obey Him as Lord.

2. Ask Jesus to baptize you in the Holy Spirit, to fill you for service. Raise your hands to Him and drink in the Spirit. Be bold enough to begin to speak the language of the Spirit that He gives you. Remember that the language of the Spirit is given to you whether you speak it or not. You should want to speak in tongues, since it helps you communicate with God and builds you up in the Spirit [see 1 Cor. 14:2,4].

3. Share what you have done as soon as possible with another person who will understand your experience.

4. Read the Scripture, asking God to make its truths as clear as possible.

5. Allow Jesus to be the foundation of your ministry from that day on.

Supernatural People

All God's people are called to be naturally supernatural. A spiritual birth caused us to be God's supernatural children, still clothed in natural bodies. The empowerment of Pentecost blesses us with supernatural power, pouring out spiritual gifts and making it possible for God's glory to be seen in earthen vessels [see 2 Cor. 4:7]. The same Jesus who poured out the Holy Spirit at Pentecost is still alive and well [see Heb. 13:8]. It is wonderful to know that He didn't stop equipping His new disciples for ministry after the first ones died. Had it all ended with them, I would be out of the ministry now. It is wonderful to know that Jesus still speaks to the church the same message that He spoke to Martha's unbelief: "Did I not tell you that if you believed, you would see the glory of God?" [John 11:40].

Many of my seminary classmates are no longer in the ordained ministry. I am sure that the greatest reason is because they lacked the spiritual power to make their ministry work. Without power a person gets ministry burnout. Good people know that God is calling them to do the work of the gospel, but it is impossible for ordinary people to do the extraordinary ministry that is required of them. God's work requires God's provision and power. This statement sums it up: *What was impossible for the early disciples to accomplish without supernatural power is impossible for us.*

It is my belief that the withering of much of the church in the United States, and in other western countries, is directly related to its inability to understand and submit to the power and direction of the Holy Spirit. I believe that this statement is true: *The church withers without God's supernatural involvement. Conversely, the church flourishes when it hears God's voice, obeys Him, and uses the means that He provides to live His life and do His work.* As the Upper Room and the baptism in the Holy Spirit were a place of beginning for me, they have also been the catalyst for the renewal of many thousands of churches. Supernatural people are being equipped with supernatural power so that they can both be and do what God expects. I have often stated that *God does not want earthly things put to heavenly use but rather heavenly things put to earthly use.* We should be less interested in what we have to offer and more in what God provides.

Pentecost Proves the Resurrection and Ascension

A wonderful byproduct of the Upper Room experience is that it confirms the truths revealed in the gospel of John. In it Jesus promised that when He ascended to the Father He would pour out the Holy Spirit upon His disciples. When the disciples were filled with the Holy Spirit at Pentecost, it proved that Jesus was truly ascended into heaven. And, if He was ascended, He was resurrected as well. The proof of this fact is repeated each time someone new is baptized in the Holy Spirit. He becomes living proof for a new generation [see John 14:29].

Luke began his Acts letter by referring to the ascension of Jesus, then reminding the readers about the promise of the Father [see Luke 24:49; Acts 1:4]. This was then connected to the baptism in the Holy Spirit. This was also what John the Baptist described when Jesus came to him to be baptized with water: "He will baptize you with the Holy Spirit and with fire" [Matt. 3:11]. This was the promise of the Father that filled his disciples with power from on high [see Luke 24:49; Acts 1:8].

Pentecost, the Resurrection, and the Ascension are inextricably intertwined. In John's gospel, Jesus foretold how He would have to ascend to the Father before the promise could come [see John 14:12–13, 16; 16:5–7]. Now He had risen and the "promise" had come. His disciples were living proof of the Ascension! Had the day of Pentecost failed to produce the "promise of the Father," there would have been no way to prove the Ascension, thus no way to prove the Resurrection.

It is when God's people go forth in the power of the Holy Spirit, in the baptism with the Holy Spirit, that the world is drawn to the risen and ascended Christ. Without the baptism in the Holy Spirit the message of the kingdom of God is reduced to words without power. With the "promise of the Father," there is positive proof that the gospel is true!

Now I Have Something to Offer

Now that my life and ministry were changed by my Pentecost experience, people were being drawn to the risen and ascended Christ. Before this experience, my words were empty of power, no life changed, no one won to Christ. Before God's intervention in my life, I had nothing to offer anyone but myself. At best, I could merely rearrange their problems and encourage them to huddle together for mutual support. I felt that I was living a lie. But now my message goes forth with the power to change lives and to win people to Christ.

Today, although many church people are languishing in similar spiritual impotency, the Holy Spirit is stirring the church—as on the day of Pentecost—to return to the Upper Room. Once again disciples are waiting upon the Lord, waiting for the "promise of the Father," the baptism in the Holy Spirit. Once again the proof of the Ascension and Resurrection is returning to the church, and people are believing God with the same convictions the new converts did on the day of Pentecost.

LEARNING TO PRAISE AND WORSHIP

The Holy Spirit Awakens Praise and Worship

"I wept aloud with joy and love; and I do not know what I should say, I literally bellowed out the unutterable gushings of my heart."[1] The nineteenth century evangelist, Charles Finney, was speaking of his baptism in the Holy Spirit. It was like receiving "waves and waves of liquid love." Its power was so great that there were no words to express the wonderful love that was shed in his heart.

"Emotionalism! That's pure emotionalism," one minister exclaimed, typical of many clergy who keep God at arm's length, lest He overcome them. This happens in many seminaries, where students are taught to believe that academics are more important than a personal encounter with God. My adviser in seminary told me to "get off that personal religion kick." Twenty-five years haven't changed things as students are led to believe that claims of personal encounters with God are somehow anti-intellectual.

How could anyone, having a direct encounter with God, fail to have a very strong emotional response? A person would have to be spiritually dead not to be awed and excited. We can go to football games and shout, wave our hands, and dance, but Christians are supposed to respond to God meekly and quietly. That's contrary to the psalmist's word to "shout for joy to the LORD . . . burst into jubilant song with music" [Ps. 98:4].

It was the excess and the shouting that almost caused Jan and me to miss out on the praise and worship blessing. We were invited to attend a charismatic meeting in Akron. This, our first foray into the Pentecostal world, came about three months after our renewal; it was not the best place to begin. The speaker was a fast-talking shouter. Despite his delivery style, I was able to be attentive to his message. But were we glad that we were sitting in the back of the room!

Upon ending his message, the speaker opened the meeting to prayer. That's when everything came unglued. People began to shout and wail, some ran up and down the aisle, some were on the floor. One woman began to scream, another to dance and shout. Our mouths dropped open as we witnessed an undisciplined mob, expressing relationships with God. They were doing their own things without any direction. Instinctively I knew that this was contrary to Jesus' command that we all be one. These people were very sincere, but their actions would certainly turn off someone seeking God. I was determined that our church would not fall into these excesses. Yet, I was just as determined that there be a way for people to express the joy of the Lord. I didn't want to quench the Spirit.

The night I received the baptism in the Holy Spirit, God's awesome presence overwhelmed me. After I had gone to sleep for a time, I woke up praising and glorifying God in tongues. Then I found myself doing the same in English, then again in tongues. The Holy Spirit had awakened praise and worship in my soul. Never before did I have such an overwhelming desire to praise and worship God. The Holy Spirit was producing God's life within me, and I was responding to his presence. Yes, my mind was responding, but so were my emotions.

The next day, while driving down the road, I had a natural desire to praise God in tongues. I even sang the praises, making up new songs. I didn't care if anyone observing me thought I was a bit odd, I just wanted to express my love and awe of God. I wanted to thank Him for what He was doing in my life. An old joke makes sense here:

There was a man who went into this church one Sunday. He walked down and sat in the front pew. That made him very obvious since other people didn't sit in front of the tenth pew back. When the minister began his boring sermon, he was greeted with "Praise God! Hallelujah!" from the man in the front row. It happened several more times, causing the preacher to lose his place. So he made eye contact with the usher in the back which said "do something."

The usher walked forward to where the man was sitting. "I'm sorry sir, but you are not welcome. You will have to leave. We can't have those kinds of outbursts here."

"But I just found Jesus," the man responded.

"Well, you didn't find Him here," the usher retorted.

Emotional outbursts of one's love of God are not appropriate in most mainline denominational churches. In these churches we often have the form of religion but not its power.

Sit in a Pew, Sing a Hymn or Two

When the gushings of my heart came forth, I began to learn the true meaning of praise and worship. I saw that liturgies, designed to enable praise and worship, had often become empty forms. Just think of this: You sit in the pew, say a prayer, sing a hymn or two, read a couple of passages of Scripture, hear the preacher talk, sing a hymn, pray a little, and go home. All must be done in one hour or less in most churches. And believe it or not, this is called "worship."

"Well, it was good enough for my grandfather, and my father, and it's good enough for me," an old-time Episcopalian told me. "I don't want some new-fangled thing in church."

It was sometime later that I thought of the response I should have given. What I wished I had said was, "Do you think that it is good enough for God?" In our egocentric manner we always see things from our point of view. We should ask ourselves the question, "Is what we call worship worthy of God?"

As other people in the church began to surrender to God and be filled with the Holy Spirit, they too had praise and worship awakened in them. The trouble was that we didn't know what praise and worship were all about. Except for following the rules of our liturgy, there was no real teaching on the matter. We didn't know what to do with people who were excited about God. Some people wanted us to squelch that enthusiasm, worried that everything would get out of hand. Finally, the experts came to our rescue.

Practicing Praise

"What I want you to do is speak praises of God for five whole minutes," the Reverend Dennis Bennett instructed our people. "Do it aloud, everyone speaking at the same time." Five minutes is a long time when you are learning to express your love of God. We had to be encouraged to continue. "Just say 'praise you, Jesus,' or 'thank you, Jesus' again and again if you run out of words." As we followed his instruction, I could sense that there was a praise power in the room. Something significant was happening. And I knew that God could hear each of us individually even though we were speaking at the same time in different ways.

Our churches are full of people who would rather that God didn't intrude in their lives. They want religion to be private, without outward expressions. They don't realize that someday, God's people will lead worship in heaven. An Anglican sage once wrote, "The first purpose of the church is to lead the choir of all created beings in the worship of God."[2] Sometimes it is fun to think of the cultural shock that will happen for many of us when we arrive in heavenly places and discover that praise and worship are loudly enthusiastic. It probably is good to begin practice now, rather than experiencing a big shock later. The door of praise and worship opens when people surrender to our Lord and are filled with the Holy Spirit.

Ten Thousand Praising God

I had such a shock when I made a trip to Seoul, Korea, to visit the Full Gospel Central Church. In those days it had 240,000 members and was still growing. Dr. Cho, the pastor, asked me if I would be willing to give a testimony at a Wednesday night prayer meeting. I never expected ten thousand people to show up, but they did! When they began to praise God it was as if every fiber of their being was involved. The sound was awesome; it was what I imagined the roar to be at the bottom of Niagara Falls. When it was time for people to stop, they had to ring bells. Otherwise it probably would have continued all night. I was reminded of this passage: "Then I heard what sounded like a great multitude, like the roar of rushing waters and like loud peals of thunder, shouting: Hallelujah! For our Lord God Almighty reigns" [Rev. 19:6].

How I look forward to that awesome day when I will witness thousands upon thousands of angels encircling the throne of God, singing in a loud voice, "Worthy is the Lamb who was slain." How glorious it will be when I join every other creature in heaven and earth to sing, "To him who sits on the throne and to the Lamb be praise and honor and glory and power, for ever and ever" [see Rev. 5:11–13]. If we allow our imagination to consider the imagery in the Scriptures, we can be left breathless with anticipation.

Praise And Worship—A Definition

As I have discovered more and more about praise and worship, I have created my own definitions as to their meanings. *Praise is the physical and verbal response to the presence of and our experience of God. Worship is our surrender to God.* Praise, thus, can be expressed in a variety of ways: song, words, painting, dance, instruments, and good works. Worship is when we surrender our selves, souls, bodies, and possessions to the will of God. Praise and worship go hand in hand.

The Unconverted Hate Jesus

"Get off this Jesus stuff," railed June (name changed). "I'm tired of you always talking about Jesus."

June didn't like it when I preached about Jesus. When I mentioned His name she stuck out her tongue at me. I tried to explain, to no avail, that without Jesus there would be no church, no Christianity. What I think she disliked was that I was making it clear that all of us needed to be in a relationship with Jesus, and that without our surrender to Him there was no worship even though we were being faithful to the liturgy.

In the Episcopal liturgy the minister says, "O Lord, open thou our lips." In my experience the congregation always gave a half-hearted response, "And our mouth shall show forth thy praise."[3] We didn't understand that the people could have begun a time of praising God, nor was there opportunity. Instead, "And our mouth shall show forth thy praise" was followed by the singing or saying of a portion of Scripture. We didn't know that the people could have entered into a time of free praise, a time of singing praise, a time of responding to God. Praise and worship demand something from the Christian, demand that we be creatively enthusiastic in our responses to God.

Our First Prayer and Praise Meeting

"On Friday we will begin a prayer and praise meeting. Anyone who is interested, please come at seven o'clock." I didn't expect many people to show up, but thirty did. I arranged the chairs in a circle so that everyone was in front, and could easily see everyone else. By this time I was able to start several praise songs, so I led the music. We didn't have anyone to play an instrument, so it was all a cappella.

The format was simple. We began by singing "Amazing Grace." Then we held hands and prayed for the people on our right, then on our left. As I led the next songs, I encouraged the participants to speak out their praises of God, both in song and word. Praying aloud was new to all of us, so we started out hesitantly but grew bolder. After we praised, prayed, and listened to the reading of Scripture, we took a coffee break. The break gave us the opportunity to have fellowship, to meet and encourage new people.

After the break, we changed our meeting place by going into the church proper. After a song and a prayer, I preached an evangelistic message, concentrating on surrender to God and being filled with the Holy Spirit. This was followed by an altar call, during which time we prayed with people to receive Jesus into their lives and to be baptized in the Holy Spirit. Then we invited people to come to the altar and receive prayer for any needs they had in their lives.

Yesterday's Blessings—Today's Boring Traditions

Those were wonderful times of growing in God, learning to be a bit more spontaneous and free in expressing our love for Him. We were moving away from two problems of worship affecting many churches— vicarious worship and fossilized worship. Vicarious worship happens when professionals are hired to worship for the people. The people don't pray because the pastor prays the long pastoral prayer or reads the prayers from the prayer book. The people don't sing praises because only the choir is called on to "sing new songs." Things become fossilized when, as one person put it, "Yesterday's exciting blessings become today's boring traditions." It is not that the traditional hymns or liturgy cannot stir praise and worship, but they often become the only fare for the people, thus robbing them of the ongoing creativity of God's people.

Sing to the Lord a New Song

"I have a new song that God gave me," Nancy said. She was one of the bolder Christians in our congregation. You never had to coax Nancy to pray, praise, or minister to people. So, when she had a song to share, I was eager to listen.

"Go ahead, Nancy," I encouraged her, "let's hear it."

Nancy began to sing, "Glorious God, I adore you; Glorious God, I adore you; Glorious God, I adore you and call forth your name in love." You could tell right away that her song was expressing things that we were feeling about our own relationships with God. Musically, although a simple gem, it would not have pleased most trained musicians. They would have called it trite, or something similar. Yet, in a very simple manner we were all led to express our love of God with a new song. I can still hear the tune in my mind. I was learning that things are new every day when we are relating to God. In a vicarious and fossilized church system, we would have been robbed of Nancy's song. Since that time, I have taught the song to many other congregations.

While there are many joys to experience when there are creativity and spontaneity, it can be very threatening to older members. Many clergy have tried to turn Sunday morning into a prayer and praise meeting without giving people the opportunity to get used to the changes. I believe that people will welcome creativity and spontaneity when their relationship with God is established or improved. However, those who are without such relationship will resist changes. *Evangelism, therefore, is the foundation of praise and worship.* When people meet the living God personally, then the church can move from stiff liturgical practices, adhering to rigid traditionalism, to creative and dynamic liturgy. We must always ask if God is pleased by the way we normally conduct worship on Sunday mornings. I think that He is bored—as are most people.

Strong Leadership Required

God gave me my wife, Jan, for many good reasons. Here's one: She recognizes, through her unease, that praise and worship are better done when there is strong congregational leadership. When people are turned on to God and want to express their excitement, they often get foolish and say things such as, "The Holy Spirit is our leader," or, "Our meeting is just led by the Spirit." This is a gross misrepresentation of the work of the Holy Spirit. People lead; the Holy Spirit guides. "The mind of man plans his way, but the LORD directs his steps" [Prov. 16:9, NASB].

When there is no strong human leadership in a church, the strong, manipulative people take control; if they don't, then the wolves (interlopers) will. Although people naturally resist authority, they can learn that it is God's way to establish people as leaders. In the worship context, a strong leader keeps things flowing in a direction, avoiding distractions. *Leadership puts the timid at ease and silences the unruly who might try to dominate the gathering.* The more spiritually dynamic church life becomes, the more the probability that there will be abuses and excesses. It is for this reason alone that strong human leadership is needed. For decades, the average mainline church existed in ignorance of the workings of the Holy Spirit; now that spiritual awakening is taking place throughout the church, we need enlightened, strong leaders.

Ruined for Boring Worship

"I can't stand that church," Ruby lamented. "It's so dead." Moving away from St. Luke's Church was often a cultural shock. St. Luke's allowed a free exercise of praise, of gifts, of prayer ministry. Ruby's new church was still fossilized in its traditions. The Holy Spirit did not seem to be welcome. I have heard from many others who left spiritually dynamic churches and found themselves in dead churches elsewhere. They were like flowers wilting because of the lack of water. When churches come alive in praise and worship, they become so wonderful that people never want to leave. It is typical that people refuse job promotions and transfers because they cannot bear to leave a church that is alive with Jesus Christ.

DISCOVERING WHERE GOD IS LEADING

In Need of Direction

At St. Luke's, we were very aware that having a vision was of first importance to parish renewal. Without vision people go their own way, not God's. Our problem was getting a vision that had meaning for the people, one that would inspire them to take hold of the future. We really worked hard at getting a vision statement, but it was like pulling teeth. I recall one vestry retreat when our leaders made a few strides in creating a vision statement.

"Why don't you just tell them where you think we are headed," challenged Ron Jackson, my associate pastor.

I don't know what Ron thought when he saw the reaction in my face. I was irritated. I didn't appreciate this young upstart dropping hand grenades into the situation. It was enough trouble just to lead the retreat; I didn't need someone blowing the process sky high. And at the same time I knew that he was right. Ron saw things that I didn't see; I needed to be challenged. I was running the meeting as if there were no leader. I wanted them to do all the work without my participation.

I know that I didn't thank Ron properly for his intervention; all I knew was that my mind was fast at work. Yes, there were things that I believed God was revealing about the future of St. Luke's. They were in my thoughts before this retreat. However, I was making one big mistake. All this time I was treating the process as a long-range planning meeting. That's when people brainstorm about what they desire for the future. You sift and collate the findings and put them in a time sequence.

Asking What God Wants

But then I realized: *If it is vision for the church, then the question is not what the people want but what God wants.* I had never been part of a church where the leaders tried to discover the mind of God, so that they could obey him. Always before it was the will of the most influential people that had to be obeyed.

Still, the process was laborious. I offered my thoughts to the other leaders. I said, "This is what I believe God would have us become and do in the future." They all breathed a collective sigh of relief. Not only was I finally leading, but what I told them resonated with things they had already been thinking. We were finally on track, finally on the way to having a vision for our future. Even so, the effort remained laborious; we were muddled. How do you envision a vision?

During this period, several other pastors and I went to a meeting with the international leaders of Youth with a Mission. They also were dealing with the problem of planning ahead. The session hit the afternoon prop-the-eyelids-open doldrums. My mind was wandering. Then it happened. I almost fell off my chair. A Pentecostal pastor from Redwood City, California, made one of the most profound statements I had ever heard. It was about vision. And I immediately thought about our struggle for vision at St. Luke's.

Four Important Vision Questions

Just what was so compelling about what the pastor shared? It was the simplicity of his formula for arriving at the all-important vision. He framed it as four questions for church leaders to answer. Here's what he said:

"We must answer the question: What kind of Christian does God expect our church to send into the world?

"Then we ask: What kind of church does it take to produce that kind of Christian?

"Third: What kind of leadership will it take to produce that kind of church?

"Finally: What kind of pastor will it take to produce that kind of leadership?"

When our congregation was working hard to produce a vision statement, we had no way to organize our thoughts, our pursuit of God's will. We were shooting, so to speak, in the dark, trying to hit the bullseye. Great amounts of energy were expended without a fruitful outcome. I was once told that the most intelligent people were those who could ask the right questions. The pastor from Redwood City asked all the right questions.

Vision about Becoming and Doing

Two major needs must be expressed in a vision statement. The first is the need for the present members to know where they are headed—what they are to *become* and what they are to *do*. When a congregation is mobilized under a common vision, people tend not to spend their time finding fault with one another. The second is the need for would-be members to know what will be expected of them if they join. Too often new members are not challenged before they join, and as a result do not easily fit in with the congregational flow.

A vision statement is that document clearly stating the outline of the congregation's marching orders and God's expectations concerning the personal lives of the members. It will express where the church family is headed, specifying what God intends them to be and what he intends them to do. The central process words are *becoming* and *doing*. Biblically, this is expressed in the Greek *exousia* and *dunamis*. In God's kingdom we are given the authority to *become* God's children and the *power* to accomplish His purposes in the world. "Yet to all who received him, to those who believed in his name, he gave the *right* [exousia] to *become* children of God—children born not of natural descent, nor of human decision or a husband's will, but born of God" [John 1:12–13, italics mine]. "But you will receive *power* [dunamis] when the Holy Spirit comes on you; and you *will be* my witnesses . . . to the ends of the earth" [Acts 1:8, italics mine].

The Redwood City pastor proposed the question, "What kind of Christian does God expect our congregation to send into the world?" Certainly God has expectations that when a person is born again into His kingdom that he or she will grow up to be more like Christ. Otherwise, the gospel is merely words without power. Many congregations

111

today never get around to challenging their people to grow in God's life. Their marching orders are never written. It is no wonder that churches die on the vine.

Being with God or Against Him

Paul knew, as all Christians should know, that God is not stupid, nor does He make mistakes [see Deut. 32:4]. He does not create anything without a plan in mind. This is true of each individual and it is true of the church. He created the church with specific purposes, promises, and plans in mind. The hope is that through the Holy Spirit's guidance and power, the church will become what God intends it to be and do what He plans for it to do. This means that the church that fails to discover and move according to God's plan could very well be living in opposition to God. Jesus said, "He who is not with me is against me, and he who does not gather with me, scatters" [Luke 11:23].

When we are in the midst of renewal or growing in God we concentrate on living in obedience to the Master. But there is no way for a church to discover God's plans apart from the person of Jesus Christ. He is the foundation stone for all that God will have us be and do. *The congregation that is not centered on Jesus will be out of touch with God and, therefore, out of touch with salvation, with life, and with the future.* Without Jesus, the congregation's growth in God is stunted or aborted and eventually overcome by mediocrity and death.

A Plan for Every Church

A vision statement enables the members to focus their thoughts and energies in the channels best serving God. The obvious assumption is that God has a will and a plan for every part of His body. Discovering that will and plan is the all-important first step in the process of obeying God. Those congregations without vision are generally forced to serve the multiple whims of its members. All of us are familiar with those congregations that struggle because of factions at war with one another.

Establishing a vision is different from doing long-range planning. A congregational vision provides the substance [God's will] and the direction [God's plan] for long-range planning. Long-range planning then helps the congregation speak of this substance and direction in terms of time, people, and resources. Once a vision outline has been prepared by the leaders and ratified by the people, the leaders' task is to develop the strategy that will enable flesh to be put on the bare bones of that vision. As the leaders prepare strategies for the future, they develop ways in which lay ministry is able to enflesh the vision.

Membership Requirements Must Become Clear

People need to know what is required of them if they are to be effective members of God's family. At St. Luke's we attempted to express to new members what was expected of them. We did this by using the following:

Q. *What is your reason for being a member of St. Luke's Church?*
A. My reason for being a member of St. Luke's Church is that God has called me to be part of this body.

Q. *What is the main purpose of St. Luke's to which you are called?*
A. The main purpose of St. Luke's Church to which I am called is expressed in a fourfold manner: Worship, Mission, Discipleship, and Community.

Q. *What do you mean by Worship?*
A. By Worship I mean that the primary calling of my life, my family, and my church is to worship God in thought, word, and deed.

Q. *What do you mean by Mission?*
A. The Mission of St. Luke's Church is to bring the saving knowledge of Jesus Christ to the world about us, beginning where we live and work. This saving work continues as we bring others into God's body and as we meet the needs of those who are among the poor and needy.

Q. *What do you mean by Discipleship?*
A. By Discipleship I mean that I am making myself available to both learn about Jesus Christ and to become more like Him.

Q. *What do you mean by Community?*
A. By Community I mean that I have presented myself to become a member of a home fellowship, offering my gifts and talents, so that I and others may be strengthened to do the work of the gospel.

Q. *What is the special mission to which St. Luke's is called?*
A. St. Luke's has been called to bring the message of the Holy Spirit's work and the renewal of the church to the Episcopal

Church and the Anglican Communion worldwide. This work is done in conjunction with many other groups dedicated to the renewal of the church.

Besides this statement, our newcomers' meetings described the general commitment of the members and what was expected of newcomers, should they join.

"We don't want you as part of this congregation unless you believe that God is calling you here. If God is calling you here, then you will come under the authority of the church leadership and the bishop of our diocese. You will be expected to tithe, or to be actively working toward a tithe. You will be expected to be part of a home fellowship that meets every week. You will be expected to share your gifts and talents so that the congregation can fulfill its vision." This was the best time to deal with new members—right up front, before they joined without commitment. However, we had to know where we were going and what was expected of us before we could call others to the same marching orders.

Without a congregational vision [direction], the people may find themselves spiritually aimless, thus serving the world, the flesh, and the devil instead of God [see Prov. 29:18]. Habakkuk heard God tell him to write his purposes down so that the people could benefit. "Write my answer on a billboard, large and clear, so that anyone can read it at a glance and rush to tell the others" [Hab. 2:2 TLB]. Successful Christians are those who are prompted to become what God wants them to become and to do what God wants them to do. Jeremiah wrote: "Set up road signs; put up guideposts. Take note of the highway, the road that you take" [Jer. 31:21].

Getting the Right Attitude

It is sometimes difficult for Americans to realize that God's church is a theocracy instead of a democracy. God doesn't ask our opinions before He tells us what is required. We don't get a chance to vote on it. This is one of the reasons that Paul was clearly concerned that congregations seek God's mind instead of the minds of the people. He was concerned lest the congregations fail to be of one mind. It is best expressed by his statement, "Your attitude should be the same as that of Christ Jesus" [Phil. 2:5]. Jesus expressed his attitude this way: "I tell you the truth, the Son can do nothing by himself; he can do only what he sees his Father doing" [John 5:19], and "I do nothing on my own but speak just what the Father has taught me" [John 8:28b].

It is not only the attitude that is important but also the mind of Christ, for it is there that we discover God's will. "Be transformed by the renewing of your mind. Then you will be able to test and approve what God's will is—his good, pleasing and perfect will" [Rom. 12:2]. It is God's desire that we come to one mind concerning His will. "I appeal to you, brothers, in the name of our Lord Jesus Christ, that all of you agree with one another so that there may be no divisions among you and that you may be perfectly united in mind and thought" [1 Cor. 1:10]. What a noble task it is for a congregation's leaders to seek God's will for their future.

The Way to God's Purpose, Path, and Provision

The *Book of Common Prayer* in describing the church says that it is one "because it is . . . under one Head, our Lord Jesus Christ;" it is holy "because the Holy Spirit dwells in it" to consecrate its members and guide them "to do God's work."[1] The Holy Spirit, keeping us on track with Jesus, gives revelation and guidance to the church. The church remains one with our Lord as it obeys the Holy Spirit. This strong connection with Jesus, the true vine, is critical because apart from Him "you can do nothing" [John 15:5].

If we are really the church, then we must be involved with the Holy Spirit, for without Him we would be rendered impotent to do God's work and helpless before the devil's onslaughts. We must always be willing to face the truth about ourselves. Are we involved with the Holy Spirit? Are we receiving from Him our purpose and plan for the future?

The church often struggles with matters of authority. Faced with the question, Who is really in charge of the church; is it God or man? Harry Blamires writes, "We know the authentic Christian voice—it is the voice of one gripped by the authority of Christianity, who wants it, allows it, to make him what he should be. We know the unmistakable heretical voice—it is the voice of one who grips Christianity by his own authority, to make it what he wants it to be."[2]

Fortunately, the church does not have to search for the Holy Grail so that it can know the will of God. "God has revealed to us already the mystery of his will!" writes Everett Fullam. "The will of God . . . centers in Jesus Christ. If we leave Jesus out of our consideration of what God is doing, we'll never understand."[3] Apart from Jesus, how can we discover God's truths and His will for the church? It is with Christ that we can discover truths hidden from ages past [see 1 Cor. 2:6–10; Col. 1:26–27; Eph. 3:2–6; 5:32].

It was God alone who exalted Jesus into such a position of authority. *Should we disobey Jesus, we disobey the Father* [see John 7:17]. *If we glorify Jesus, we glorify the Father* [see John 13:31; 14:13]. "He is before all things, and in him all things hold together. And he is the head of the body, the church . . . so that in everything he might have the supremacy. For God was pleased to have all his fullness dwell in him" [Col. 1:17–19]. Our divine marching orders come from Jesus, in whom the fullness of the Father dwells. When the church's pastors, priests, vestries, boards, and elders understand that they have divine marching orders, they will no longer serve the will of empty theology or of competing factions. With such obedience to Jesus Christ, they will never be accused of loving "praise from men more than praise from God" [John 12:43]. Simply stated, *the church does not seek the collective mind of its people, but the single mind of God.* An obedient body is much more pleasing to God than anything else the church might achieve [see 1 Sam. 15:22].

Learning to Hear God

"What I want you to do is go out in the woods, sit down someplace, and listen to God. Don't talk at Him. Just listen. When He talks to you, then write it down."

There were uneasy snickers, shocked looks, and disbelief among the forty people who attended the retreat. God talking to them? The fact that many had been raised in a Christian environment did nothing to minimize their consternation. They just didn't believe that it was possible for God to talk to them. In their minds, God was like a watchmaker who wound up the universe and then sat back to watch it tick along.

"No, I'm not kidding. When you get where you are going, tell God that you will listen to Him. When He speaks to you, then write it down."

I sent them off to listen to God.

At the appointed time they wandered in, each seeming to hold on to something precious.

"Who would like to share what God spoke to them?"

There was a long silence as no one seemed willing to be the fool who said he heard God speak. I waited them out, looking at each person.

Then as it always seems to happen, someone raised a hand. I nodded and the person began to read from her pad. Once the ice was broken, the rest shared their precious notes from God. Some were shared in tears as God had spoken profound things into their lives. Others received direction for the future. But all had something to share!

Personal vision is similar to a congregation's vision. God speaks things telling us what to be and do. It helps to ask the right questions of God, such as, "Lord, how do you want me to change, and what is the first step?" Or, "Lord, what is it that you want me to be doing?" There are many different ways that we can hear from God, for God is a communicating God. The book of Hebrews describes God's communication this way: "In the past God spoke to our forefathers through the prophets at many times and in various ways, but in these last days he has spoken to us by his Son" [Heb. 1:1-2]. Here are some ways for God to communicate His purposes to us:

1. *Through Scripture.* Not only does God speak through His written Word, but the written Word also becomes a test for the authenticity of other words attributed to God. God will not speak contrary to Scripture. A congregation should encourage people to "read, mark, learn, and inwardly digest" God's written Word.

2. *Through the Congregation's Leaders.* When God calls people to be leaders of a congregation, He also prepares them to hear or sense His special Word for that parish. For instance, the Antioch church leaders heard God say, "Set apart for me Barnabas and Saul for the work to which I have called them" [Acts 13:2]. Some people call this a *rhema,* a word for directing us today. Our situations in congregations are no different. When we agree to listen to God, then we will be most able to hear. Whether we hear audibly or in our inner self, it makes no difference. What is important is that God has spoken and we have heard.

3. *Through the People.* God, of course, interacts with the people daily. Sometimes He will speak things that affect the entire congregational life. The leaders are responsible to hear what God is speaking through the people. One of the best ways to hear from God is to open meetings up so that people can share what they experience and hear from God. The leaders are then responsible to judge the word as to its

source, whether from God, the person's mind, or the devil. Practice will perfect this process.

4. *Through the Things God Does.* When God changes lives, heals, and sustains, He is also sending clear messages concerning the present direction of the congregation. When He is active, He seems to bless what is happening. When He is inactive, He seems to be withholding His blessing. Although that latter point is not always true, it helps to be aware of God's actions in a congregation.

5. *Through Outsiders.* God often speaks to us through things other people write or through conference talks. No congregation should try to shield itself from that which God is importing from the outside. This caution will be a safeguard against the temptation to believe that only we can hear from God.

Again, if we help people focus on the right questions, then what we hear will be more focused. The responsibility of leaders is to compile, sort, and put in outline form what God is saying to the congregation.

Since many church people do not understand that God is speaking to them personally, they need to be encouraged to listen to Him. They need to be instructed about how to listen and what to do with what they hear. As a congregation's members begin to discover that God has special plans for them and for their parish, they need helpful instruction and practice to discern his voice. "'For I know the plans I have for you,' declares the LORD, 'plans to prosper you and not to harm you, plans to give you hope and a future" [Jer. 29:11]. "For we are God's workmanship, created in Christ Jesus to do good works, which God prepared in advance for us to do" [Eph. 2:10].

The Four Questions Applied

I have taken the four questions that the Redwood City pastor gave and added to them so that we can focus fully on what God has in store for us.

About the Individual Christian

Leaders ask: What kind of Christian does God expect us to send into the world? What does God expect each Christian to do in the world?

People ask: What kind of Christian does God expect me to be?
What does God expect me to do?

About the Congregation

Leaders and People ask: How must our congregation change so that we produce God's Christians?

What must we, as a body, be doing to fulfill God's general and specific will?

About Parish Leaders

Leaders ask: What kind of leader must I be to align our parish with God's will?
People ask: How can I encourage our leaders to obey God more effectively?

About the Pastor or Head of the Congregation

Leaders and People ask: What kind of clergy will produce the most effective leadership?

The People Must Ratify the Vision for It to Be Meaningful

Any vision begins small and is expanded as time passes. It is as Jesus spoke to Paul, ". . . what you have seen of me and what I will show you" [Acts 26:16b]. A vision statement grows as people grow and *has no authority until it is ratified by them.* Sometimes leaders make the mistake of pushing something onto people, as if the leaders are the only ones who can hear from God. Spiritually smart people reject this effort to dominate. As time passes, a vision statement will change, broaden, and provide more goals for the parish. In any case, a vision is essential to the healthy future of any congregation, for without it the people will languish [see Prov. 29:18]. They may disobey God even as they do good things. God calls us not to do good things but to do God things. When we are doing God's things then we are both radical and supernatural.

Seeing the True Church

It is very important to see the church in the manner God intended. There is no secular language that can adequately describe the

119

supernatural church. We cannot examine and characterize its institutional structure, and we cannot portray it by its physical structures. The supernatural church can only be described through the various revelations of the Holy Spirit expressed in the lives of Christians, both now and throughout history. The church is a people who have been formed and given life by the Holy Spirit. It speaks of a radical way of life in which people are called to make radical commitments to God and to one another. It is the *ekklesia* (Greek for "church") which has been called out of the world so that it may be prepared to be sent back into it as God's ambassadors. The church was never meant to be understood as a mere man-made agglomerate but as the supernaturally constituted body of Christ. It is a community in which the Holy Spirit operates—a union of God and man.[4] There is no other creation like it in heaven or earth.

It seems strange that our true identity can be hidden from us. We are like the story of the king's daughter who lived with another family. It was not until her true heritage was revealed that she had the opportunity to fulfill her potential. Christians have been baptized into God's promises, but few know who they actually are and what it means. They need to hear the message and then take possession of their birthright. Gaining God's vision for the church restores the church to that birthright.

Even before I entered seminary, I had trouble understanding the supernatural church. I understood the term "body of Christ" as describing the "man-made agglomerate" that I was experiencing. "Supernatural" was not a word I normally used, except to describe goblins and ghosts. It is no wonder that I expected little of the church upon entering seminary. I learned to expect even less after receiving instruction there. Even though I served on the vestry of a church before seminary, my experience was that the church was no better than a civic club.

Now I know that it is possible for God's people to inquire of Him, to ask very direct questions and to get very direct answers. Because such inquiry of God is not typical to normal church experience, church people must be converted, filled with the Spirit, taught, and encouraged before things change. There is one thing that is always certain: *God has a will for every congregation and desires to make it known.*

LEARNING TO RAISE UP LAY MINISTRY

A Lesson from Moses

"I can't continue to do all the counseling that I have to do," I complained to our leaders. "I have far more people to see than hours in which to see them."

This was the second time that I made this plea. I did it a year earlier, without any helpful response. Now things were more serious. I was wearing myself out; burnout was just around the corner. I knew that my situation was no different from that of most clergy. We try to be all things to all people. It seems to be an inbred problem: when someone calls, we answer the phone and make ourselves available for whatever the person perceives his need to be. The main difference for me was the steady increase of members that multiplied the perceived needs.

I don't blame our leaders for not responding favorably to my previous lament; they were only responding in the way they had been taught. Ministers are hired to do ministry for the congregation. My friend, Terry Fullam, always liked to say, "The minister ministers while the congregation congregates." If this is the way most churches are run, could anyone be expected to understand it any other way? If you pay someone for a job, then he ought to do it. Why should our leaders be responsive to my complaining?

"I am suggesting that we turn the ministry of counseling over to laypeople. After they are trained, we can shift the responsibility to them."

This time the response was very different from the first. It was the difference between shocked amazement and head-nodding acceptance. I had done my teaching job well, for they now understood that the work of ministry belonged to laypeople. Two accounts in Scripture helped me come to an understanding in this matter. The first concerned Moses and the second was Paul's letter to the Ephesians. For clergy, these could very well be the most important career aids available. From them I learned to ask some hard questions: What ministries are so sacred that only the professionals can do them? Has God set apart any work for clergy only? If so, what?

My enlightenment began as I read about Moses' encounter with his father-in-law, Jethro [see Ex. 18]. Every clergy person needs such a father-in-law. Jethro listened well to Moses' account about all the things "the Lord had done to Pharaoh," the hardships, and "how the Lord had saved them." He "was delighted to hear about all the good things the Lord had done for Israel." Jethro not only listened, but he tagged along as Moses did his ministry. This is where the light came on for both Moses and me.

What Jethro observed when he tagged along with Moses was something that a clergy person's father-in-law might see if he tagged along in church. Moses began his job and the people "stood around him from morning till evening." This was typical of so many days that I spent doing the clergy thing. I had appointments throughout the day. I had to prepare things to teach and preach. There were hospital visits to perform, meetings to lead, and people who would call in the middle of the night. When Jethro saw all that Moses was attempting to do he said, "What is this you are doing for the people: Why do you alone sit as judge, while all these people stand around you from morning till evening?"

I could have given Moses' response: "Because the people come to me." Somehow I believed that I was some type of Christ figure. In hindsight I know that it was more of an ego trip. I felt good when I helped someone. I gained an inner satisfaction knowing that people sought me out for their problems. At times I even believed that God called me to St. Luke's Church for that very purpose. I learned that my motives for serving people were not always pure. There were times when I could tell sympathetic members of our congregation how I hardly slept for days and how last night I never got to bed because of a crisis. "Because the people come to me" is a dumb rationalization for continuing to wear oneself out.

Jethro gave Moses the perfect response. "What you are doing is not good. You and these people who come to you will only wear yourselves out. The work is too heavy for you; you cannot handle it alone." He hit the nail on the head. If the leader of the church is overworked, becomes tired, and finally burns out, then the congregation will also be hurt. They will respond to the situation in unhelpful ways. Their stress will increase, they will become tired, and they will pull away from involvement. What Moses was doing, what I was doing, and what clergy continue to do today just does not make good sense. There has to be a better way.

Jethro was not only critical of Moses' situation, but he was ready to offer helpful advice. He told him to appoint other leaders to do the work of ministry—except for the hard cases. His main job would then be to watch over the leaders and see that everything was done properly. Because Moses was serving God, Jethro added, "If you do this and God so commands, you will be able to stand the strain, and all these people will go home satisfied." Jethro knew that God would approve of such a ministry change. Jethro knew that the people would "go home satisfied."

We learn in the Numbers 11 account that Moses took the problem right to God. Jethro must have stirred Moses to the truth about the situation. He says to God, "What have I done to displease you that you put the burden of all these people on me?" At times, this is exactly the way I felt. When I was so tired that I could hardly think straight, my emotions got in the way. I was tired and making the people tired. Moses needed help and now he knew it. God responded, echoing Jethro's advice, "Bring me seventy of Israel's elders who are known to you as leaders . . . They will help you carry the burden of the people so that you will not have to carry it alone." But God added, "I will take of the Spirit that is on you and put the Spirit on them." Whatever the spiritual anointing was that enabled Moses to do his ministry was the same spiritual anointing that would be given to the people. When God calls people to do things for Him, He equips them for the work.

Obediently, Moses selected the seventy elders to be anointed for ministry. They were then given the Holy Spirit, gifted with supernatural power for the work they were called to do. As Moses saw what God was doing, he said something profoundly prophetic: ". . . would God that all the LORD's people were prophets, *and* that the LORD would put his Spirit upon them!" [Num. 11:29]. He looked forward to the coming of Christ and when the Holy Spirit would be poured out at Pentecost. He looked forward to the supernatural equipping of all God's chosen.

All Ministry Open to All

I made a list of twenty duties that could be given over to laypeople, but I kept it to myself for a time. I think I would have scared our leaders off if they knew that I was seriously considering empowering laypeople for the following:

1. Calling on new and old members.
2. Evangelizing the unsaved.
3. Visiting the sick and shut-in.
4. Being a confessor.
5. Counseling the emotionally and mentally distraught.
6. Crisis counseling.
7. Grief counseling.
8. Feeding and caring for the poor.
9. Administering discretionary funds.
10. Praying for healing.
11. Being leaders over ministries.
12. Teaching new people.
13. Conducting worship.
14. Conducting Bible studies.
15. Praying for deliverance.
16. Leading small fellowship groups.
17. Administering the church.
18. Discipling others.
19. Teaching at all levels.
20. Closing the doors and turning out the lights.

"But what did *you* intend to do?" That was the question someone would ask if he read the list. I was already teaching my answer; it just wasn't time for my full list. I was starting with just one item.

Ministry before Gifts

Notice what Paul tells us about church leaders in Ephesians 4:11–12. The reason God gifts the church with leaders is so that they can prepare God's people for works of service. The people are called to do the work of ministry, and leaders are called to prepare them for that ministry. Isn't it wonderful that Paul recognized how churches ought to run?

By this time, St. Luke's people were ready to hear this teaching.

They had committed their lives to serving God; they had their Upper Room experience of the Holy Spirit; now they were ready to do ministry. In fact, many had come to me, telling me that they felt called to ministry. I began to understand the urgency of responding to them. I now knew that my job, as an ordained leader, was to open the doors for ministry and to prepare the people for it. It is my belief that if we had a true every-member ministry in place, few persons would want to go on and be ordained, for they would have a full ministry without it.

Up to this point, many wonderful Christians were being denied the opportunity to use spiritual gifts because there was no provision for ministry. We had already "made the mistake" of encouraging people to "discover their gifts." We were reading books about spiritual gifts, one in particular encouraging people to begin the discovery process by filling in worksheets. Sure enough! People saw themselves as having spiritual gifts. Frustration ensued! There was no place for people to use their supposed gifts. We as a congregation were not yet open to lay ministry. Besides that, we didn't know enough about gifts to describe them adequately, let alone discover them. I remember one teacher making gift discovery easier by relating gifts to those things people liked to do. This only confused people because I was teaching them that spiritual gifts are supernatural and are supernaturally imparted.

Finally the light dawned. I realized that spiritual gifts are never one's possession, and that gifts are seldom experienced apart from the performance of ministry. It is in the midst of serving others that we discover God at work. It is then that we are presented with opportunities to exercise spiritual gifts. When we do ministry we rely on God, and then become channels of his grace. When Peter and John [see Acts 3:1–10] were going to the temple to pray, the opportunity for ministry appeared. The lame man became the ministry opportunity, and as Peter obeyed the Holy Spirit, he became a channel for God's gift of healing.

Spiritual gifts are never our possessions, not something we own. During ministry, God puts in the minister's hands gifts to be given away. At the conclusion of ministry he or she should be empty of gifts. Performing ministry thus releases spiritual gifts. My experience is that I never know ahead of time what God is going to do, or what gifts He will impart. Our work is to go where the Holy Spirit leads us. When we get there, then we are to do what He does and say what He says. Thus, Jesus' saying comes true: "Anyone who has faith in me will do what I have been doing. He will do even greater things than these" [John 14:12].

I never would have said that Helen had a gift of healing. But God gave her a ministry in which a man was healed. Art had come to the altar rail for prayers. He could hardly kneel from the pain in his back. A couple of us laid hands on him, asking God to heal him. When we were finished, he was no different. Now, our service was ended and Art was on his way out the door when Helen came up to me and said she believed God wanted to heal Art. I told her to run after him and bring him back for prayer. Art obediently returned. This time Helen and a couple of others sat him in a pew and prayed for his healing. Suddenly, his body was filled with warmth, and he was healed on the spot. Helen was given the ministry opportunity. She had a word of knowledge that opened the door, and when she prayed with Art a gift of healing was imparted.

Preparing the People to Do Ministry

The church leaders who heard my complaint about my counseling schedule were ready to do something radical. It was decided that I would see to it that some laypeople were prepared to counsel people; when they were ready, we would tell the congregation that I was no longer doing counseling. The laypeople would be given the opportunity to show what they could do. It is ironic, I thought, that I was given no preparation for counseling people, yet people treated me as if I were an expert. But the laypeople needed training.

After several months the first group of laypeople were ready to become counselors. I even had a laycouple who took upon themselves the main responsibility of seeing that people were prepared. The leaders and I stood before the congregation and explained that from now on I would not be doing any counseling and that the laypeople would. The congregation members were told that they would be asked, if they called for an appointment with me, what their reason was for wanting to see me. If it was for counseling, then they would be shifted to a layperson. What was the result of all this? The laypeople did a wonderful job of counseling, and the congregation got used to going to them for help. I remained faithful by not taking appointments, even though the temptation was great to give in to someone who tells you that he needs you.

Testimony Tells of the Spirit's Presence

We were finally lighting the Spirit's fire by increasing the work of ministry. Although there had been testimonies of God's work among us, increased ministry increased the testimonies. Testimony is a sign of God's life in the midst of a congregation. If there is no testimony to give, then there is an absence of God's abiding life, an absence of the Holy Spirit, and an absence of people fully committed to Jesus Christ. It was John who said, "That which . . . we have heard, which we have seen with our eyes, which we have looked at and our hands have touched—this we proclaim" [1 John 1:1]. If God is at work through ministries in a congregation, then there will be stories to tell, stories of God's supernatural involvement with the people.

Jesus said to Nicodemus, "We speak of what we know, and we testify to what we have seen" [John 3:11]. Anything less would have been deceitful, for testimony involves experiences with which a person is familiar, not something about which one speculates. It is important that church people be led deeper and deeper in relationship with Jesus Christ, for only then will they gain the experience of God about which they may testify.

It is easy to establish a religious institution that has the right creeds, the right liturgies, and the right leadership but which has little or nothing of God's life. Ministries, and the gifts imparted through them, help change this. When a person receives something from God, there is a testimony to give. When many people are receiving from God, there is a greater testimony to give, greater assurance of God's life among them. I began to understand how important it was for there to be a time to give testimonies on Sunday morning. Otherwise, there is no way for people to know that God is at work, no way for their faith in God to be increased or strengthened.

Ministry Principles

As time passed, simple principles about ministry began to emerge. *First, ministry is the servant work to which every Christian is called.* Ministry provides opportunities for God's love to be shared with His family. God calls us to begin perfecting this loving activity at home before we try to export into the world what we have not experienced. It is the object of Paul's words, "Therefore, as we have the opportunity, let us do good to all people, especially to those who belong to the family of believers" [Gal. 6:10].

Second, ministry has two major ingredients, the natural and the supernatural. Often God will call us to use our natural and learned gifts and talents to bless others. Yet, it is God's intention to infuse our natural selves with Holy Spirit power through the baptism in the Holy Spirit. If we do ministry only with our natural gifts, it may fall short of God's expectation. We must learn how to exercise supernatural gifts of the Spirit, for only God knows when they are to be used. Perfect ministry happens both when natural ministry is infused with spiritual direction and power and when supernatural gifts flow freely. We must, however, always remind ourselves that spiritual gifts are not our possessions, since we are merely used as the channels for them.*

Third, supernaturally infused ministry imparts God's life and love to the recipient. Natural ministry, though temporarily helpful and good, is still temporal. It cannot be valued as highly as that which comes from God. Supernaturally gifted ministry helps babes in Christ to mature and to grow in supernatural kingdom life. Jesus said it this way: "Flesh gives birth to flesh, but the Spirit gives birth to spirit" [John 3:6].

Fourth, supernaturally infused ministry is essential to every local congregation. Without God's supernatural activity there will be little growth in Christ, little shedding of old life and living in the new, little fruit of the Spirit, and few new disciples. A church body that does not feed on spiritual gifts will be stunted and will eventually wither on the vine and may someday be pruned away. Spiritual fruit grows from spiritual roots and spiritual nourishment. The people then become more loving "as each part does its work." They will be prepared "for works of service" because they have attained "to the whole measure of the fullness of Christ," and have grown "up into him who is the Head, that is Christ" [see Eph. 4:12–16]. When people grow in God's life, ministry is multiplied manyfold, and the process is repeated as they enter into ministry.

Fifth, the church that releases ministry manifesting both spiritually empowered natural and supernatural gifts is a church that will attract others into the kingdom of God. Such a church will be faithful to the Great Commission to make disciples; it will minister to the needs of both the people of God and the people of the world. As I heard a preacher once say, "That's a dynamite situation."

Many of us came into God's church because we had an encounter with God. Some had this experience as small children, teenagers, or in the military during wartime. These experiences often were so awesome that we feared telling others about them. Clergy who once had super-

---

I have used the term "channel" several times. The reader should not confuse this with "channeling" practiced by New Age religion, which is abhorrent to God.

natural encounters with the Holy Spirit may have set them aside in their attempt to be more theologically sophisticated. They may never have shared their experiences with their flock. Yet, all of these experiences point to one thing, to the supernatural activity of the Holy Spirit in our lives. God in His wisdom and grace chose to meet us, to create a divine encounter, and not without purpose. God does not waste Himself. Some of us, however, never returned to seek more from God, or to discern His ultimate will for our lives. In that case, Paul has a question for us: "After beginning with the Spirit, are you now trying to attain your goal by human effort?" [Gal. 3:3].

All True Churches Are Charismatic

The unfortunate tag *charismatic* has been attached to those experiencing the present-day outpouring of the Holy Spirit. This term is often used to imply that the rest of the church is not charismatic. This notion is neither biblically nor theologically correct. The word *charismatic* comes from the Greek word *charisma,* meaning "gift." When referring to the present outpouring of the Holy Spirit, it describes the spiritual gifts that constantly are being bestowed upon the authentic church. It would be better for the modern day charismatics to use the term to indicate that they are being obedient to the Holy Spirit. As Christians have no control over Him, they can only go where He goes, say what He says, and do what He does.

The root for *charisma* comes from *charis* which means "grace." Grace is a free gift which God lavishes upon us, a most wonderful gift to enjoy. One of the most beautiful words employed to describe the Lord Jesus Christ is that he was "full of *grace* and truth" [John 1:14]. Paul cries out in a moment of ecstasy, "Thanks be to God for his indescribable *charisma*" [2 Cor. 9:15].[1] The authentic church is God-formed. Could there be any authentic Christian who made himself that way? Can the church claim anything as authentic that the Holy Spirit has not brought to life? The answer is no! The church by its nature is charismatic, or at least it should be.

God releases within the church various manifestations of the Spirit through gifts, service, and working. Paul said it this way: "There are different kinds of gifts, but the same Spirit. There are different kinds of service, but the same Lord. There are different kinds of working, but the same God works all of them in all men" [1 Cor. 12:4–6]. The words *gifts, service* and *working,* though rendered differently in different translations, still have the same meaning. Spiritual gifts are given to all believers for the building up of the body of Christ. The word for "service" is *diakonos,* which is the same word used to describe those New Testament believers who were set aside to minister to the needs of the church. It is wonderful to know that all Christians are given the spiritual power to function as servants. Jesus said that those who wanted to be great in God's kingdom needed to become servants of all [see Matt. 23:11].

Energema is the Greek word for "working." *Energema* refers to our ability to perform the works of God [see Eph. 3:20]. In 1 Corinthians 12:10 it is used to describe a gift of working miraculous things. Jesus had already promised that the believer would have abilities to do even greater works than He, so this was not a new idea [see John 14:12]. Performing the works, along with other manifestations, provides a wonderful combination for the Christian. We could sum up Paul's word in First Corinthians by saying: *God has promised that we will be able to achieve the works of God with loving servants' hearts and with the perfect gifts for our ministry.*

Spiritual Gifts Lead Us Toward God's Will

Once, during a time of crisis, our leaders were reflecting the mood of the whole church by being fragmented and disheartened about what was happening to us. Resentment and mistrust abounded. There was a lack of common direction. At a retreat, the Lord told us that we should become repentant before him, confessing all of the things we were thinking and feeling. After we had done this, we waited upon the Holy Spirit to show us what to do next.

"I believe the Lord is telling me to pray and anoint each of you." I was sure that I was hearing the Holy Spirit on my insides. The leaders all stood around the room as I began to pray and anoint each one. When I came to the first person and put my hands on him, the power of God came, and the man fell back into his chair. As I touched each one, the same thing happened. They could not stand in the presence of the Holy Spirit. But as each person yielded himself to the Holy Spirit, lives were changed, attitudes were changed. Then God began to manifest his gifts through various people. We soon gained a new direction, more united as one body.

Next, we gathered over ninety other leaders who were also struggling. We called them to repentance and waiting upon the Spirit. As the

Holy Spirit came into our midst, mighty things began to happen. God poured His gifts upon us. Soon reconciliation and healing started to occur. At the end of the evening there were scores who had been delivered, healed, and strengthened. It seemed that no one was the same. Each went back to his duties with renewed spiritual vigor. Had not the gifts, service, and working been released, we might still be struggling.

Releasing lay people into ministry did not make our congregation perfect or problem-free. That was never the idea. What it did do was enable us to respond better to God's leadings. The lay counselors did their work so well that nearby clergy referred their people to us. At one time our case load was over one hundred. Not all counselors were the best, but they were as good as most clergy anywhere. Besides the counseling ministry, after a year or so we had over two hundred and fifty of our congregation engaged in meaningful ministry.

Spiritual Gifts Build the Body of Christ

Our congregation had awakened to the reality of supernatural gifts of the Holy Spirit. We listened to Paul who said, "Eagerly desire spiritual gifts" [1 Cor. 14:1]. We learned not to fear spiritual gifts, as many seem to do, fearing misuse or excesses. It is only in the midst of our experience of the manifestation of the Spirit that we gain understanding and alleviate our fear. David Watson said it simply: "The answer to *misuse* is not *disuse* but *right use*."[2]

The baptism in the Holy Spirit and spiritual gifts are part of God's provision for the supernatural life of the church. Ministry, through which spiritual gifts come to life, enables the people to be edified and changed. Fruit of the Spirit is born as God's life becomes increasingly incarnate in and through us. In simple terms: no ministry, no gifts, no fruit. The Holy Spirit provides the only means by which we can do God's work effectively. Paul, using a very persuasive argument [see 1 Cor. 12:12–26], tells us that each part of the body of Christ has tremendous importance for the whole. God has so arranged his people that each spiritual gift is essential for everyone's growth. When the gifts are being manifested, there will be ongoing sanctification, or growth in God's kingdom.

Start Small Without Haste

When it comes to ministry and spiritual gifts, practice makes perfect. Getting started with ministries and gifts can be one of the most exciting endeavors that the leadership of a congregation can undertake. It is exciting because it is new, and it is potentially full of God's life. It is just for this reason, however, that a congregation should proceed without haste. There is no need to rush things if you carefully follow a plan. Here are some ideas:

1. *Test everything on the leadership first.* Begin with your board of elders or vestry, then your other major congregational leaders. Meet weekly, after making a covenant with one another, to learn more and more about ministries and gifts. Have experts come in to help you experience supernatural gifts.

2. *Follow a detailed plan.*
   a. Pray that each person will surrender his or her life to Jesus Christ. Seek a way to do this together. Lay hands on one another to bless the decision.
   b. Pray that each person will be baptized in the Holy Spirit. Pay special attention to my chapter concerning the Pentecost experience. Encourage each person to speak the language the Spirit enables.
   c. Create a plan for your leaders to jointly visit a congregation involved in spiritual power ministry or attend a power ministry conference.
   d. Make an inventory of those ministries that could be put in lay hands immediately and of those that could be given over at a later date.

3. *Then answer these questions:*
   a. Who is called to do each ministry? Pray and ask God. Have the people pray. When they know and you know, then make the choice. See it as a trial run.
   b. What preparation will the person need in order to begin? Who will disciple the person? Is it necessary to have an outsider come to assist in the preparation?
   c. Is this a ministry that takes risking, but no formal preparation?
   d How should the congregation be informed about this new lay minister?
   e. Will the leadership give this person the authority that must accompany the responsibility?

4. *Once chosen and prepared, formally commission the person for the ministry.*

5. *Set up a way to monitor the progress of each minister.* Be sure that there is an appointed leader to whom the person is responsible.

6. *Always ask the question, Is the right person doing the ministry?* Be willing to change things rather than having the wrong person languish.

7. *Meet regularly to talk about the progress of the ministries.*

God Gifts a Barren Woman

Every ministry, every gift that is manifested, has a small beginning. Someone had to risk doing what he believed God wanted him to do to start. He had to put one foot ahead of another. He had to risk making mistakes. At one service, I remember getting the impression in my mind that God wanted to enable a barren woman to have a baby. I fought with the idea, wondering if I really heard from God. "What will the people say," I thought, "if there is no barren woman present?" But finally I knew that I had to go obediently where I thought God was going and to say what I thought He would say.

"I believe that there is someone here who has tried to have a baby for many years, but you are unable to have children. Would you please come for prayer, for God would like to heal your condition." I risked being a fool.

"Thank you, God," the young woman said as she knelt down. "We have tried and tried, we have been everywhere, spent tons of money, but we still can't have children." Tears came down in huge drops.

"I thank You, Jesus, that You care for this woman. I thank You that You have sent forth Your Word, telling what You intend to do. Now, Lord, remove this barren condition and enable her to become pregnant." A few months later I heard from this woman's pastor that indeed God had healed her; she was now pregnant. I have thought since that she may never have been healed unless I had been obedient to follow the Holy Spirit's leading.

So it is with every congregation. We as leaders do all we can to lead people to be obedient to God by taking on the ministry He puts before them. Then we encourage them to be responsive to the Holy Spirit by manifesting the gifts of the Spirit that He makes available for the ministry.

15

LEARNING TO LIVE IN FELLOWSHIP

Mistake After Mistake

Talk about mistakes!

I often wondered how many mistakes are allowed before God pulls the plug. Without someone to help us learn about Christian fellowship, our attempt was like being on a raft, drifting about, hoping to find a place to land. Our first real fellowship group was made up of the people who responded to the call of God on their lives. When we had thirty-five people, it was very meaningful; we all knew each other, our concerns, needs, and victories. Those were such wonderful days. But it couldn't last; our congregation was growing. After awhile we didn't know each other, our concerns, needs, and victories. This is where the mistakes began.

It was dawning on me that we needed to create small-group life if each person was going to be ministered to in ways that used to be possible. The need was epitomized by my encounter with Rhonda (name changed).

"Why are you abandoning us? Why are you dropping us as friends? All you do is pay attention to the new people."

I knew why Rhonda was so upset. When she and her husband surrendered their lives to the Lord and became members of our congregation, I spent a lot of time with them. I visited them in their home often, and they were very kind to me. But now they had matured in their Christian walk, and I had to spend less time with them and more with new Christians who were coming on board.

"I'm terribly sorry, Rhonda, that I have offended you. I never intended to do so. Will you forgive me for my offense? I won't be able to change the way that I deal with new members, however. I still must spend most of my time with them."

"No, I won't," was Rhonda's response. And then she added a few other choice words.

A mistake had already been made in the way we gave pastoral care; now we were paying for that mistake. What was it? We failed to provide small fellowship groups as entry-level places for new people. We failed to offer ways to receive pastoral care other than from me alone. We needed fellowship groups from the beginning of our renewal. The people needed relationships; they needed family.

I love Psalm 68:6 which says, "God sets the lonely in families." Whenever Jesus spoke about being a son, He did so from the perspective of His family relationship. That relationship was so important that Jesus spent time relating how He and His Father were One. When we think of the family of the Trinity, we cannot avoid bringing to mind the relationship of the Father, Son, and Holy Spirit. This fellowship was so important that Jesus prayed that we, the church, would experience similar unity [see John 17:21–23].

Such *koinonia* (Greek for "fellowship") is not natural to us, but rather, arises out of our shared experience of the Trinity [see 1 John 1:1–3]. God forms us into His supernatural family, thereby enabling us to come together in spiritual fellowship. At the same time, He provides operations and gifts of the Spirit so that we can relate to one another in real life. Because *koinonia* is not natural to us, it is something into which we must be converted. We must see the possibilities spiritually, in our hearts, and commit our lives to live out *koinonia* with others in the church.

I was gaining the right perspective a day late and an hour short. In the church it is hard to undo mistakes. The new perspective was great; I was learning that the church, by its nature, gathers into its fold fragmented, downtrodden, disheartened, lonely, and spiritually impoverished people. All of us need God before we come. It is through the blood shed on the Cross that we become blood relatives. No longer must a person live a solitary life without a family. The wonderful thing is that we have God as our Father, God the Son as our brother, and God the Holy Spirit as our companion. I learned that it is impossible to have fellowship with many people at one time; we are forced, by necessity, to establish our primary *koinonia* with a smaller group.

Mistake Number Two! You would think that after you get the picture and begin forming small fellowship groups that everything would be great. Wrong!

"I know that you have enjoyed our fellowship time together," I told a group of men. They were some of the more mature Christians in our congregation. "I think that it is important for us to begin forming many groups similar to this one. I want you to pray about becoming the leaders of these new groups."

It sounded like a very innocent beginning. It had the best of intentions, good people, and an idea that was overdue. I was not prepared for the trouble that would eventually come of it. First, some of those to whom I had given this new responsibility were not capable of doing it; they really weren't leaders. They tried, but they were either too overbearing or not assertive enough. It wasn't long before their groups died. Some of the leaders did rather well, the group members developing lasting bonds. But there was one who was very good at it. His group grew to be thirty, then fifty, and finally over sixty! The leader was dynamic but not disciplined. The group, under his leadership, began to be a counterforce to what we were doing in the rest of the church. This group existed for itself. I was worried that these people might even begin their own church. I did everything I could to remove as many from this group as possible.

Mistake Number Three came when we tried to correct Mistake Number Two. My associate, Ron Jackson, had some experience with cell groups, which he called house churches. He said that if we really wanted to do things right, we had to make house churches the main emphasis of our church life. He suggested that everyone should be involved, and that I, the rector of the church, should push on it very hard. The idea Ron suggested was attractive because it would deal with the problem that our runaway group presented. In the house church format, the leaders would all be committed to the fulfillment of the parish vision. They would be much more disciplined and would be submitted to the leadership of the church. I wasn't so anxious to make a change this time; I wasn't ready to jump in with both feet until I saw success. I wanted to see his ideas tested without the entire parish being involved. I told Ron that he could gather some people together and train them to be leaders of house churches.

What Ron did was not the mistake. He went at things in the right way.

Meeting with the twelve people on a weekly basis, he taught them how to lead small groups, about being a pastor who meets the many needs of the people, about how to lead worship, about how to lead inductive Bible studies, and how to encourage people in their walk with God. During the six months they met, the leaders practiced their skills on one another. Soon they were ready to start their own groups. That process was simple. We announced the formation of the groups, revealed the leaders, had a large meeting and those who came opted for the group with which they wanted to be associated.

As the house churches began, everything seemed to be great. Soon, I put my other foot into the process, encouraging everyone in the congregation to be part of a group. The clergy and wives even began their own group. But Mistake Number Three was lurking at the door. It just took several months before we heard its knocking. The house church leaders were oblivious to the problem; they were enmeshed in what seemed to be a great ministry. They didn't know that small-group death was lurking at their doors.

When Ron taught the leaders, he told them that they needed to reach out and evangelize others, bringing them into their groups, lest they dry up. After several months it had become apparent that none of the groups was making evangelism a priority. This proved to be a huge problem for us as the groups were much like previous ones—they *didn't add new members*. How strange it was. The only previous group that grew in numbers was the one that wasn't submitted to the leadership of the church. In fact, their numbers came from the members of the church, not from making new converts. The house churches were supposed to reach out to the unchurched and make new converts. In both of our attempts there seemed to be a reluctance to do just that.

Reasons Why People Don't Want New Members

Groups develop several reasons why they don't want new people to join them:

1. *Lack of readiness.* They need to get their lives in order before they will be ready to take on new people.
2. *Chemical imbalance.* New people will ruin the chemistry of the group.
3. *Lack of openness.* People who have openly shared their lives in the past will no longer be as open.

4. *Always at square one.* They will always have to present basic material to the new people, thus not allowing for the spiritual growth of the older members.

5. *Lack of intimacy.* More people will take away the intimacy possible with a smaller group. (Note: Original source unknown.)

Each one of these excuses squeezes spiritual power from the groups. If people wait until they are perfect before they reach out to others, they will never do it; they will only be perfect when they go to be with the Lord. Also, it destroys the understanding that God takes imperfect earthen vessels and enables them to do supernatural things—not because they are ready, but because they are submitted to the will of God.

When groups worry about their chemistry, they subtly tell you that they are too advanced to share what they have with anyone else. What began in the Spirit is now continuing in the flesh. They are like selfish husbands and wives who do not want children because it will interfere with their romance. They won't be able to spend as much time together, or have special moments—the children will change everything. They will never be able to recapture what they once had. The chemistry excuse is similar to the excuse that groups are better when they can openly share their lives—their problems, concerns, fears, past. New people make this openness virtually impossible, they contend. Often these groups never grow in God's life because they spend so much time rehearsing the past and present problems. If they have grown in God's life, then they have mistaken their openness as the catalyst of change instead of the Holy Spirit. Besides that, they say that real problems need tender loving care best handled by those who are better prepared for the task.

A lot of people worry about always having to be at square one because new people require basic teaching. It is when we have gone past square one that Scripture tells us we should now be teaching others. Those who are not teaching others always need to go back to square one so that they can learn enough to teach others. Once they start teaching others they will begin to learn the deeper truths that God wants them to understand. We are disciples first so that we will be able to disciple others. When new people come, the group gets larger. This allows some of the more mature people, who are not yet leaders, to take part of the group and form a smaller one. In this way, disciples learn to be leaders and are then given the opportunity to practice what they have learned. As long as groups continue to divide into smaller groups, there should be no fear that there will be a lack of intimacy.

Applying Pressure for Groups to Evangelize

"For some time, each of you has been leading or assisting in house church leadership."

I was speaking at a regular meeting of leaders held every quarter. On this particular occasion, I hoped to inspire them to reach out and evangelize others, as it was apparent they were not doing so.

"Tonight, I am here to encourage you and your groups to reach out and evangelize others. Turn with me to Psalm 69." As I led them to read portions of this psalm, I had them pay close attention to phrases such as "for the waters have come up to my neck," or "I have come into the deep waters . . . I am worn out calling for help."

"Throughout the neighborhoods around you are people who feel like they are in a sinkhole. They have struggled in life until now they feel as if they will sink even deeper until the water covers them up." They all knew what I was talking about because many of them were in such a state before a friend came to rescue them, leading them to the Savior and helping them to discover a new life.

"Think about those people who have been praying this prayer for many days now, perhaps weeks, months or years. 'But I pray to you, O LORD, in the time of your favor; in your great love, O God, answer me with your sure salvation. Rescue me from the mire, do not let me sink; deliver me from those who hate me, from the deep waters. Do not let the floodwaters engulf me or the depths swallow me up'" [Ps. 69:13–15]. I encouraged them to know that all around them people are praying for a Savior. They are desperate for someone to come and rescue them. "Who will care enough to reach out to them?" I challenged the leaders.

"Now turn to the fifth chapter of Luke. Notice a couple of important things in this familiar story. The men had been fishing but hadn't caught anything. Jesus told them to put out into the deep water. Notice the term *deep water*." Then I showed them that they were fishing in the wrong places—in shallow water. Jesus took them right to the place where the harvest of fish was ready.

"When they got into deep water, they caught more fish than they could handle. Then Jesus likened their experience to that of evangelizing people. 'Don't be afraid; from now on you will catch men.'" Some of the leaders were beginning to see the light. "Now turn to Matthew

11, right at the end. We say this passage in our Rite One Communion service. 'Come to me, all you who are weary and burdened, and I will give you rest.' It is Jesus' intention to reach out to those whose lives are weary and burdened, for He has a way to bless them.

"Now turn back to the ninth chapter of Matthew; this is one of the most important passages that you will ever read. Verse 35. Notice Jesus' work here. 'Jesus went through all the towns and villages, teaching in their synagogues, preaching the good news of the kingdom and healing every disease and sickness.' We are called to be doing identical things— spreading the good news about God's kingdom and making people's lives whole. Now read on. 'When he saw the crowds, he had compassion on them, because they were harassed and helpless, like sheep without a shepherd. Then he said to his disciples, "The harvest is plentiful but the workers are few. Ask the Lord of the harvest, therefore, to send out workers into his harvest field."'" I could tell that things were sinking in.

"Where is the harvest field?"

"With the harassed and helpless," someone volunteered.

"Why fish in shallow water when God has prepared a harvest in deep water? God is saying that we will not have any trouble reaching out and evangelizing people if we go to those who are already searching for God. Their lives are troubled; they need a Savior. You know people all around you whose marriages are failing, families are in trouble, they have messed-up lives, and so on. Why not reach out and bring some of them to God?"

One of the house church leaders immediately identified their main asset. Many of their group had been involved in bad marriages that had been healed and changed by God. They also knew of several people in their neighborhoods who were suffering with bad marriages. Goals were soon set for them to reach out and see what God would do. This house church quickly grew in size as the members began to harvest those people in deep waters. It was necessary for them to divide into two smaller groups. The same leaders then grew another group to a size that spawned a new house church.

Some Groups Still Not Convinced

Unfortunately, the other house church leaders did not follow the example of the successful group. If they had, many new cells would have been formed, giving more and more people the opportunity to have meaningful Christian fellowship. As Samuel Butler wrote: "He that complies against his will, is of his own opinion still." Our leaders were of the same opinion. Some of them did grow slightly, but in general they were resistant. Although many of them enjoyed their continuing fellowship, they failed to heed the command of our Lord to make disciples.

They failed to understand that God never intended that people gather in community or fellowship to serve their own needs or ends. True fellowships, born of the Spirit, will find themselves serving both one another and those to whom God leads them. A true fellowship will bring "baby Christians" into being by reaching out with the gospel message. "Baby Christians" will need to huddle together for edification and comfort, for growth and inspiration; but the mature will find themselves being drawn to "Jerusalem, Judea, Samaria," and wherever they are led.

Principles of Fellowship

John, in his first epistle [see 1:1–4], gives us the secret of being full of joy. It is revealed when we share with new people our fellowship with God the Father and with Jesus Christ his Son. The gift that God gives is a gift that must be shared with others in order that we may experience its fullness. *Koinonia* begins when we enter into relationship with God. We have a fellowship with God that produces joy. We have *koinonia* with each other because we are related to the same Father. We are family. However, the Father's desire is that his family increase in size. He commissions us to search the highways and byways seeking those who want to be part of God's family. We proclaim our experience of God so that others may "have fellowship with us."

A principle of fellowship is: *We cannot have fellowship with one another unless together we have fellowship with God.* We might believe that we benefit from close warm fuzzy personal relationships with each other, but we cannot grow in Christ unless together we are submitted to Christ. This means that we make ourselves available to the Holy Spirit to be led in whatever direction He desires. The key, therefore, to good Christian *koinonia* begins when we join hands to be in submission to the will of God as revealed through Jesus Christ by the power of the Holy Spirit. I have known people in many groups, formed with the right ingredients, who have allowed their relationships with each other to take precedence over their submission to God. Submission to God means sharing what they experience with others. It means discovering the joy of seeing others have the joy to be found in Jesus Christ.

Another principle of fellowship is: *We cannot have fellowship with God if we are unwilling to include others in our fellowship.* Real fellowship expresses itself with a balance of the outward and the inward. It reaches outward to the pagan world to share the kingdom of God with the lost and the helpless. It reaches out to show the love of the Father in good works. Fellowship expresses itself inwardly by being devoted to God's Word, to growth in His love, to healing, to worship, and to sharing. When the balance is intact, then the community will renew itself as God works through the fulfillment of its mission and as the members receive gifts of the Spirit within.

A third principle of fellowship is: *True Christian fellowship always releases an abundance of spiritual gifts that enable the people to grow in God.* Every Christian is given supernatural gifts to give others. The exercise of these gifts enables people to mature as disciples until they are ready to lead others in their growth.

A fourth principle of fellowship is: *Every fellowship meeting needs a trained leader who is full of the Spirit and wisdom.* A wise trained leader keeps people on the right track, growing in God and fulfilling the mission of the larger body. We must always be careful not to assume that an untrained person will be able to successfully lead a fellowship group. It is more difficult to remove an ineffective leader than it is to choose and train the right one in the beginning. The success of fellowship groups depends on leaders chosen for the task.

A fifth principle is: *Every leader needs continuous oversight.* Everyone who leads others needs some system of accountability so that all are assured that they are being led in the right direction. It is easier for people to submit to a leader whom they know is submitted to others.

A sixth principle is: *Every leader needs the authority necessary to carry out the responsibility with which he is entrusted.* Churches often fail in their efforts to get lay ministry going because they do not give the lay leaders the authority necessary to carry out their work. Pastors often retain the authority in fear that they will lose control. Training leaders and inspiring them to fulfill the mission of the church usually solves the problem and keeps them on the right road.

A seventh principle of fellowship is: *Start small.* Successful groups start with the leaders available and with those who are willing to start a new ministry. This means that experimentation occurs with a few groups, not with larger and more unmanageable ones. Learning to have fellowship groups means that changes will be made till everything is working well. Once a few groups get it right, then an all-out campaign can be undertaken.

A Reasonable, Holy, and Living Sacrifice

Fellowship or community-building must proceed through the supernatural involvement of the Holy Spirit. Without such divine involvement, the family of God would lose its *koinonia.* Suenens says, "Living the Christian life means essentially to allow Christ to become the common life shared by Christians. It is to leave the Spirit free to build the church in us in the diversity and convergence of his complementary gifts."[1] God has given the church the gifts of the Holy Spirit for its edification. Thus, the grace of God is poured out in supernatural ways and the grace-full church participates in this outpouring of God's love. Augustine said that "through the one Gift, which is the Holy Spirit, there is a distribution to the community of all Christ's members of many gifts, appropriated to each of them."[2]

The responsibility of the church is to inquire of God for the meaning and purpose of *koinonia* in this day. At the same time, the church must avail itself of all that the Holy Spirit wishes to do to form it into a dynamic body. The power of the church will be demonstrated as it willingly obeys the leadings of the Holy Spirit. "And here we offer and present unto thee, O Lord, our selves, our souls and bodies, to be reasonable, holy, and living sacrifice unto thee."[3]

16

LEARNING HOW TO CHOOSE LEADERS

Servant or Leader?

"I don't think that we should call anyone a leader!!"

"Why not?" I asked.

"Because we are not called to lord it over people; we are called to be servants instead."

"But you allow people to call me a leader."

"It's because you're ordained. You went to seminary. But I don't *like* to call you or anyone a leader."

"Look, the church cannot be run by a committee. That's not God's way. Otherwise, He would have done something differently about apostles, prophets, evangelists, and so on. You know that all through biblical history, God has raised up people to lead others. Otherwise, His will wouldn't be fulfilled. Isn't that true?"

"Yes, but . . ."

"Weren't the apostles called to be leaders?"

"Yes, but . . ."

"And hasn't that been true all through Christian history?"

"Yes, but there have been abuses."

"Sure, there have been abuses. That's because we are human beings who are still being perfected. None of us is without fault. But if we must wait for perfection before we can become leaders, the church will never fulfill its mission. We all need to be servants, but some of us are called to be leaders of others. And of course, we are not called to lord it over people but rather to treat them as Christ would."

All Begin at the Foot of the Cross

"Brothers, think of what you were when you were called. Not many of you were wise by human standards; not many were influential; not many were of noble birth. But God chose the foolish things of the world to shame the wise" [1 Cor. 1:26–27]. *God chooses the sinful, foolish, weak, lowly, and despised to carry out His mission on this earth.* What else could be meant by these words: "I have not come to call the righteous, but sinners" [Matt. 9:13; see Rom. 3:23; 1 Cor. 1:26–29; Luke 7:47; 15:2; Rom. 9:16]? In God's kingdom we all begin in the same place—at the foot of the cross and in need of God's love, compassion, mercy, and forgiveness. Thus, we are chosen, not because we have anything to contribute to God's kingdom but rather because He loves us enough to provide the means of reconciliation. This is truly an amazing love. "Amazing love! How can it be that Thou, my God, shouldst die for me?"[1]

One of the most difficult things for me to handle was not to accept the call to ordained ministry but to visualize myself as a leader. I was prone to see others as more mature, more eloquent, more educated, more holy, and so on. This tendency was often reinforced when I came into the company of other clergy who seemed to be head and shoulders above me in Christian stature. I was often amazed to hear people rave about my teaching, telling me how good it was and how it affected their lives. When I was in the company of older and more mature people, I often perceived myself to be a young boy. It took a lot for me to risk being a leader of them.

God chooses people to become leaders from among those disciples who began at the foot of the cross, not from those who have excellent resumés full of qualifications, status, natural gifts, achievements, personality, looks, or possessions. Instead, God chooses leaders from those whose hearts are bent towards Him, those who desire to obey His will and be His ambassadors in this world. He looks for disciples whose hearts, minds, and wills are being molded by His hand, those willing to rely on His supernatural provision for ministry and leadership.

I have never liked the "pretty" pictures of Jesus, for they do a disservice to the rest of us. They make Him look as if he had everything going for Him, not like a normal human being. I am always encouraged by

Isaiah's picture of Jesus, "He had no beauty or majesty to attract us to him, nothing in his appearance that we should desire him" [Isa. 53:2]. It is natural for us to want a king who is tall, handsome, intelligent, and gifted. This was the mistake that the Israelites made when they asked God for a king. They didn't want just anybody that God could anoint to be king; they wanted Saul. Saul was "an impressive young man without equal among the Israelites—a head taller than any of the others" [1 Sam. 9:2]. Later, when David was chosen to replace Saul, God revealed his method for choosing someone: "The LORD does not look at the things man looks at. Man looks at the outward appearance, but the LORD looks at the heart" [1 Sam. 16:7].

The Wrong Way to Select Leaders

At my first vestry meeting at St. Luke's, I was introduced to the way church people choose their leaders.

"I nominate Henry; we need an attorney on the vestry."

"And I want to nominate Sue; she hasn't been in church for some time. This might be a way to get her involved." I doubt that anyone saw the shock on my face. I was thinking that Sue's nomination was the dumbest thing that I ever heard, an outright stupid way to choose leaders. No one else seemed to be bothered. No one seemed to care what God might think.

Since God is choosing ordinary people to be faithful in leadership roles, the church must become very sensitive to the Holy Spirit so that the leaders selected are those whom God is choosing. Otherwise, everyone will suffer. This means examining people through God's eyes [see 1 Cor. 2:10–16], knowing that if their hearts are right, then they will be pliable in God's hands [see Matt. 6:10; 26:39; Luke 1:38; James 4:7].

Leaders Are Submitted to Authority

A Christian leader is, by definition, a person who is submitted to authority. First, there is a personal submission to God that expands with a mutual submission to the elders or authorities of the church [see Eph. 5:21; 1 Cor. 16:15–16; Heb. 13:17; 1 Peter 5:5]. Christian leaders cannot be effective unless their lives demonstrate the fruit of God's life through obedience to His will. As Jesus was submitted to the Father, they are submitted to Jesus through the interaction of the Holy Spirit.

One cannot say, "I am only submitted to Jesus, and that's all that is needed." The circle is completed when one submits also to those in authority in the church [see Acts 16:4]. We must always beware of those people who want to pontificate but are not submitted to any authority. Christian leaders demonstrate their willingness not only to follow Jesus and to be transformed by Him but also to accomplish His will in the world. Paul said, "Follow my example, as I follow the example of Christ" [1 Cor. 11:1].

God Chooses Some Before They Are Ready

I remember one man who, when converted to Jesus, had to repent of an old life that clung to him like glue. Women, bad debts, gambling, and years of going in the wrong direction had covered his life with heavy scales. Getting rid of them took years. But his heart was right before God. I saw God at work in him even though his outward life did not yet conform. I knew that someday he would be a church leader. To me, Denny was a living example of a treasure in an earthen vessel. When I considered him, I tried to fix my eyes "not on what is seen, but on what is unseen" [2 Cor. 4:18].

Others did not see what I saw. They were impatient because his growth in God took so long. Even Denny thought he should be a leader before his time. I just waited, knowing that his day would come. And as sure as God is faithful, Denny emerged like a butterfly as his new life began to be expressed in his everyday living. Today he is a respected church leader and family man. God chose him for leadership years ago, and since his heart was pliable in God's hand, he became a strong leader in God's kingdom.

Leaders Are Committed to the Mission of the Church

Leaders are not only converted *to Jesus* but also *to the body of Christ* and its mission. They are converted to and understand the fact that the church is supernatural and expect that God will demonstrate His supernatural power in and through it. Leaders are also committed *to full every-member ministry* within the church, trusting that God will supernaturally work through the ordinary person.

"When Jesus had called the Twelve together he gave them power and authority to drive out all demons and to cure diseases, and he sent them out to preach the kingdom of God and to heal the sick" [Luke 9:1-2].

Throughout biblical history, as I have stated, God has consistently selected some people to lead others. When He had a plan in mind, He chose a person to carry it out. The leader, having been called, was then prepared and empowered by the Holy Spirit so that he or she could complete the work that God had in mind. Calling, preparation, and empowering are still essential for anyone God calls to a leadership role in His church. One of the problems we had in appointing leaders over fellowship groups was that we called them to the task but did not prepare them. By violating God's plan, we doomed some of the groups to failure.

Those Called Must Be Empowered

We are more familiar with God's *calling* of church leaders than we are with His *empowering* them. Most sermons have concentrated on the *call,* using texts such as, "Leave your country, your people and your father's household and go to the land I will show you" [Gen 12:1]. "So now, go. I am sending you to Pharaoh to bring my people the Israelites out of Egypt" [Ex. 3:10]. "Then I heard the voice of the LORD saying, 'Whom shall I send? And who will go for us?'" [Isa. 6:8]. "While they were worshiping the LORD and fasting, the Holy Spirit said, 'Set apart for me Barnabas and Saul for the work to which I have called them'" [Acts 13:2].

Unfortunately, it is possible for people to slip into ordained ministry without a clear call from God. They may choose church "service" as one might choose being a doctor, lawyer, or electrician. These people often consider themselves *professionals.* In England, in times past, the male's position in the family determined whether he would enter church service. The eldest son followed in the father's footsteps, the next went to sea, and the next became a priest. Yet the only true claim that those seeking ordination should be able to make is that God is calling them to such leadership. We should naturally reject those who have no *call.* Otherwise, the empowered leader is absent from the church. As important as a *call* is, we must always be aware that we are all prone to self-deception; thus, a person's *call* must be tested and confirmed by the leadership of the church.[2]

Leadership Traps

When considering a person for leadership, Michael Harper says that the church should be wary of three dangerous traps.

The first is to select someone for leadership merely because he or she has been faithful for a long time.

The second is to select a person to represent some interest group within a parish.

The third "is to be afraid of what people will think of us if we pass them over."[3]

Our experience at St. Luke's Church adds a fourth trap when considering lay leadership. It is to fail to select a person because there is a fear about designating a lay person as a "leader." Leadership, whether ordained or lay, is a true servant ministry ordained by God. People are called to it for the benefit of the congregation. That is why it is essential that leaders always serve, not dominate. Because the exercise of power is part of church life, leaders must be on guard so that they don't abuse that power, for that would be the opposite of service.[4]

The early disciples learned from Jesus, through both word and example. It was a *show and tell* operation, which is what discipleship is. This is the problem with the seminaries I have known. They generally tell but do not show. In fact, if they had to demonstrate the power of what they were teaching, there would be less taught. Discipleship puts people on the cutting edge of Christian life. That's what Jesus did with the disciples. He took them out of the world and put them on the cutting edge of the kingdom of God as it penetrated the kingdom of darkness around them [see Acts 26:16–18; Matt. 4:16; John 1:5; 3:19; Eph. 5:8; 1 Peter 2:9].

Leaders Are to Be Discipled First, Educated Second

God prepares all Christian leaders in the same fashion, but instead of discipling through Jesus, He disciples through church leaders. This is the basic role of clergy—discipling those who are being called into lay leadership. Then the process repeats itself. These new leaders begin to disciple others in the congregation. Unfortunately, the church makes the mistake of trying to give disciples and potential leaders a seminary education rather than discipleship training. There is a vast difference. Leadership is not as simple as putting principles to work for God. It certainly does not mean dispensing erudite ideas to the people. If a person is to be an effective leader, then God's principles must be written on his or her heart. When this happens, a person's life will naturally conform to God's will. Good discipleship training helps people get the principles in their hearts so that they may demonstrate them in their behavior. It was for this very reason that the early church picked leaders from the ranks of those who had already matured as disciples [see Acts 6:3].

The methods of the early church seem to conflict with the way we choose leaders today. We appear to be more concerned with education than we are with proven ministry and maturity. We choose those who will perpetuate the *traditions* of the church rather than the *tradition* of the apostles. We are concerned with a person's mental health, academic qualifications, and *lack* of zeal. Christian zeal is seen as "narrow," "not balanced," and as some in our denomination say, "un-Episcopalian."

Christian maturity demands not only that a person's heart is changed by the Holy Spirit but that his or her mind and actions are transformed also. A mature disciple will shine as a light on a hill for all to see. A potential leader must have a life that is *radically different* from both non-Christians and immature Christians. The early church saw the unchanged Christian as being immature, not ready for major ministry [see Heb. 5:11; 1 Tim. 5:22]. As the early church expressed itself more fully on this matter, guidelines for a mature life began to appear. It is my belief that these were intended as guidelines and not rigid rules, that they were something into which one matured [see 1 Tim. 3:1–13, Titus 1:5–9]. If they were intended to be rigid rules, none of us could be leaders.

Think how frustrating it would be to be sent by God on a holy mission, but not to be given the necessary provision to do it. It is like asking an artist, because she has good hand and eye coordination, to be a brain surgeon tomorrow. In my travels throughout the church, I have met many clergy who feel terribly frustrated. With great expectations they began what later was revealed to be an impossible task. And so it is! *Leadership and ministry in God's church are impossible without divine provision.* Biblical examples abound. Moses was told, "When you return to Egypt, see that you perform before Pharaoh all the wonders *I have given you the power to do* " [Ex. 4:21, italics mine]. Paul felt the hands of Ananias, an apparent novice at that kind of ministry (he expressed fear), touch him; and then he was "filled with the Holy Spirit" [see Acts 9:10–18].

Dispensational Teaching Robs the Church of Gifts

"But the gifts of the Spirit are not for today. Things have changed since the apostles' times. They were given spiritual power as a sign. It was necessary then. We don't need it because we have the Bible. That's what our Baptist pastor told us, Chuck."

"Where does he find that in the Bible?" I asked. It was obvious that they were distressed. They only went to their pastor to share with him how God had blessed them with the baptism in the Holy Spirit. He promptly threw them out of the church.

"It's the part about 'when the perfect comes.' He says that tongues and gifts have ceased and that the perfect has come in the form of the Bible."

"I'm sorry that this has happened to you. He obviously is not paying attention to the Scripture; rather, he is only mouthing a teaching that someone gave. Anyone reading the passage carefully will conclude that the perfect means Christ. Sadly, your pastor is doomed to frustration, for he is denying the very provision designed to make his ministry successful."

This teaching, called "dispensationalism," is common among groups such as Moody Bible Institute and Dallas Theological Seminary. Its teaching stresses the idea that the baptism in the Spirit and speaking in tongues lasted but a short time; the same is true of other gifts of the Spirit.[5] That period was one dispensation, while the present dispensation is evidenced by the written Word of God.

During the ensuing months, several Baptist families came to join our congregation after being ousted from their own. When these pastors deny the existence of spiritual gifts, they remove the power that makes the gospel good news. By reducing Christianity to mere teaching, they fall under Jesus' word to the Sadducees about being in error because they "do not know the Scriptures or the power of God" [Matt. 22:29].

The church must thank God for the presence and Pentecostal power of the Holy Spirit. Without it we could not be God's people, nor could we do what God's people are supposed to do. The early training mission of the twelve disciples demonstrated God's intention for the church of the future. He sent them out with "power and authority to drive out all demons and to cure diseases . . . to preach the kingdom of God and to heal the sick" [Luke 9:1-2]. Before Jesus left his disciples after the Resurrection, he told them to remain in the city until they had been "clothed with power from on high" [Luke 24:49]. Thank God that when He calls us into His kingdom and then sends us forth, He provides us with the same power, for the same tasks. It is still God's intention that we drive out demons, cure diseases, heal the sick, and preach the kingdom of God.

Nothing has changed in the church except our expectations. The impotent church does not expect its leaders and people to be empowered by the Holy Spirit. It does not understand the baptism in the Holy Spirit, nor Jesus as the baptizer. The dynamic church, however, expects and experiences the fullness of the Spirit's power, especially through its leadership. This is not a "second experience" but a primary filling with the Holy Spirit for ministry. Power for ministry is the promise. Impotent ministry will describe its paucity; powerful ministry will declare its presence. Some leaders have been robbed of their rightful provision because of poor teaching. That is why I encourage all people to seek what Jesus, the baptizer with the Holy Spirit, has available for them. "How much more will your Father in heaven give the Holy Spirit to those who ask him" [Luke 11:13b]. Yes, there is only one baptism for the forgiveness of sins; it is performed by the church with water. But there is the baptism that Jesus does; it is in the Holy Spirit for ministry power.

Enfleshing the Church's Vision

The work of empowered leaders is to help the people put flesh on the vision of the church. They not only provide leadership in gaining a vision, they empower and lead people to enflesh it. The obedient church is the active channel through which God may do his work. That's God's way; He is not searching for a sacrificial church, but rather an obedient one. This was clearly stated in the Old Testament when He declared that He would rather have obedience than sacrifice [see 1 Sam. 15:22]. Leaders help the entire church bend its will toward God's. God wants to be the builder of the church. "Unless the LORD builds the house, its builders labor in vain" [Ps. 127:1]. In fact, Jesus told us that anything that God does not establish will fail to prosper and may even come to destruction. "Every plant that my heavenly Father has not planted will be pulled up by the roots" [Matt. 15:13].

Beginning the Discipleship Process

Leaders can be discipled anywhere: in weekly meetings, through sermons, Bible studies, teaching seminars, counseling, conversations over lunch, discussions over dinner, breakfast meetings, or impromptu visits to people at their work. The *where* and *when* of discipleship training is not as important as the *what*. Those doing the discipling must find out and teach what the people need to know, not what they want to tell them. A leader who listens to God and who relates well to the people will be one who will cause the greatest growth in those disciples.

I was driving to the airport; my passenger was John Sherrill, who wrote *They Speak With Other Tongues* among other books. I wasn't about to arrive at the airport without picking John's brain.

"John, how do you decide what you are going to write in a book?"

"I don't decide what I am going to write," he answered. "I try to find out what people need to hear, and then I write that."

This was an amazing insight for me. I immediately thought of the way that I prepared sermons. Until that time, I always made a decision about what I was going to tell someone. I didn't realize that often this is a veiled hostile or judgmental activity. It certainly wasn't a pure motive for being a preacher. With the new insight, I began to concentrate on discovering what people needed to hear, what God wanted them to know. I noticed the difference in people's response almost immediately. They began to hear God in what I spoke instead of hearing me. But the temptation is always there to tell someone something. I constantly meet clergy who are bent on getting their message through to the people.

For instance, a leader knowing that certain people in his congregation do not know Jesus may decide to preach a message telling the people that they are all sinners and that they will die in their sins if they don't confess that sin to God. He may preach this message well, give the people an opportunity to respond, and be perplexed when there is no response. By all outward appearances, he has done a great job—good illustrations, great scripture references, and outstanding delivery. He may even conclude, because of the lack of response, that the people are rejecting God. The truth, however, may be entirely different. Perhaps in God's plan the people needed to hear another message. Maybe they needed to hear a message about what it means to surrender one's life to God. Had this leader spent time inquiring of the Lord, he might have communicated the right message and gotten the hoped-for response.

Giving lay people books to read is always very helpful. Some of the most helpful are:

Basic Christianity by John Stott

Called and Committed by David Watson

Nine O'Clock in the Morning and *The Holy Spirit and You* by Dennis Bennett

Kingdoms in Conflict by Charles Colson

Evangelism Through the Local Church by Michael Green
Miracle in Darien by Bob Slosser
The Christian Mind by Harry Blamires
Out of the Saltshaker by Rebecca Pippert
Power Evangelism by John Wimber.

Each book has its own character and message. If people are going to read these, they might need a time and a person with whom to discuss each one. As you give a book to a particular individual, pray that it will provoke the understandings and insights that will help that person grow in God.

There are thousands of audiotapes and videotapes that can be helpful in the discipleship process. Most churches that are in the process of renewal tape sermons and teachings and make them available for sale. A parish committee, consulting with the pastor, could amass a library for use within a parish. The committee could listen and evaluate, thereby eliminating problem teachings. Testimony tapes are door openers, helping evangelize people.

Clergy can use the pulpit to teach. It is best, unless you are an exceptional preacher, to discover simple messages people need to know and teach them. Don't look for fruit too quickly. Remember that it takes an entire season for a tree to bear its fruit. What is the season in your church? How long will it take before what you teach begins to bear fruit? Don't be impatient either with yourself or with others. Just use every opportunity at your disposal. Teach and continue to teach.

Laymen too need to become biblical thinkers. Taking a Bible to church is an excellent idea. In this way, they can follow along as the lessons are read; and they can make relevant marks in their Bibles as they listen to sermons. By doing this, they will develop their own potential teachings should the day come along that they assume leadership roles.

Just as Jesus began with a few disciples and captured the world, clergy must begin with a few people rather than attempt to change an entire church at once. Many clergy have smashed themselves on the walls of resistance merely because they tried to make everything happen immediately. They were not content to start in a small way. I once heard of four criteria that a missionary organization used:

1. *Begin small.*
2. *Trust God to fill in the vision.*

3. *Put finances in a secondary place.*
4. *Everything under God depends on the leadership selected for the task.*

There is great wisdom in these four concepts. Jesus told us that if we can be trusted with a small responsibility, then we can be trusted with a larger one [see Luke 16:10]. When I first entered business, before I was ordained, I sold houses in a small subdivision. After I proved that I was responsible in this job, I was offered a larger responsibility. When I proved myself in that one, I was given even more responsibility. I believe that the Holy Spirit will lead us to take small steps, learn to do the job well, and then He will lead us to do even more. That's how we learn most easily—step by step. The vision of any church will grow as God fills in the blanks. As leaders show that they are faithful, God will add to the vision that will guide people into the near future. Finances, of course, always seem to bother congregations that have few disciples. But as more and more people are discipled and as more and more people become leaders, there will be an increase in finances. We should be careful never to allow finances to set the agenda for the future of the church. God always provides for what He calls into being.

Finally, leaders are of utmost importance. Choosing the right leader for a task will make the difference between success and failure.

17

ENTERING INTO
CHURCH RENEWAL

Demanding the Best

"Why is it that people leave their brains behind when they become church leaders?"

"What do you mean?"

"I mean that a business wouldn't hire a manager or foreman if that person had no experience. And when they did hire someone, they would expect them to produce. Otherwise, they would be fired."

"I take it that you think we are rather lax."

"Lax is not the word; negligent would be a better one. We put people in charge of committees and then don't hold them accountable. I don't remember the time we fired someone for doing a bad job. These are the people we have representing us in the world. The non-Christians must think that we lost our brains when we surrendered to God."

"I understand what you mean; but the argument is made that this is a volunteer organization. We depend on the good will of the people to get our Christian workers. They are also the ones who give the money. If we offend them, they might pick up their marbles and go someplace else."

"Then we ought to let them go. If people don't care to do the best job possible, they shouldn't be put in positions of responsibility. I believe that we offend God when we don't demand the best of every Christian."

He was right! We should demand more of people than business and industry does. We should be training people well before giving them responsibilities. Then we should hold them accountable to do the best job possible. All of this needs to be done with the greatest possible love and concern for the individual and for his or her growth in Jesus Christ. Later, similar conversations with this friend about the way we conduct church business would take place. Each time I gained more and more insight into the ideal church arrangement.

As time passed and I gained more experience with a renewing parish, I began to see that a good place to begin getting things in order is with *the overall parish vision*. We needed to know if we were on the right track or not. We had already experienced many mistakes and dead ends that we didn't need to experience. It would have been helpful if some-one could have pointed the way, given us some way to understand what we were doing, and warned us of possible pitfalls. In other words, we needed some way to know if we were being successful.

The Doorway to Renewal

All renewal begins with Jesus. When we only know *about* Jesus and are not converted to Him, we will at best be nominal Christians. It is important to believe that God is not pleased with nominal Christians. The remedy for the nominal Christian is to be evangelized and con-verted. Church leaders must always be very clear, understanding that there will be no church renewal until people are converted to Jesus Christ. If we are to be effective in renewal, our minds must be changed in these ways:

1. *We must believe that God is not pleased with nominal Chris-tians.* It is not enough merely to claim salvation because of one's baptism and faithful church attendance.
2. *We must believe that Jesus is the doorway to God's life.* There is no other way.
3. *We must believe that every Christian must be converted to Jesus Christ.* Otherwise that person will not enjoy kingdom life.

We tend to make far too many assumptions about the spiritual health of people, and about the benefits of infant baptism.* In actual fact, the

*I am very much in favor of infant baptism but out of favor with current practices which convey the idea that baptism somehow magically conveys spiritual life to the one being baptized.

spiritual health of many baptized people is dismally bad. If it were good, our churches would be vibrantly alive, full of powerful Christians willing to give their lives for the sake of the gospel. Our churches would be growing in size and in God's life. It is not judgmental to acknowledge the truth.

I had the shock of my life some years ago. I led the service in an Ohio town to help the rector who was on vacation. After the service, since it was the local custom, I went with some of the people to breakfast. One of the men sitting next to me began to brag.

"You know, I have never missed an eight o'clock service here for seventeen years."

"Is that right?" I responded.

"But I'm not a Christian," he said proudly.

Since that time, my surprise has changed to dismay. There are many more like him throughout the church.

All renewal begins with conversion to Jesus. It is foolish to try to create renewal symptoms such as praise, fellowship groups, lay ministry, gifts, etc., without the catalyst for renewal, Jesus. Those who try to bypass Jesus will eventually fail in their renewal efforts. Here is an example.

"I'm so discouraged I don't know what to do," Jim, (name changed) a fellow pastor, lamented. "I tried introducing renewal songs on Sunday, but people got angry. Then, I introduced the idea of our vestry operating in unanimity rather than voting, and that went over like a lead balloon. Now there are some people who are opposing me through a telephone campaign."

Jim's head hung down and his lip quivered. I really felt bad for him. But this was a story that I had heard before. I was ready with a question.

"Tell me, Jim, how you have gone about evangelizing the people?" I already knew the answer, but I felt that it was necessary to stress the point I was about to make. Jim had attended one of the Parish Renewal Institutes that we held at St. Luke's. He heard me stress the fact that renewal begins with evangelism. I explained that the clergy will circumvent evangelism and try to take a back door into renewal. I warned them that it would fail.

Jim stared at the floor before he answered. "I thought that I would try the other first. Anyhow, I don't know how to do evangelism." He forgot my telling the clergy that if they couldn't do evangelism, they should either learn how or get someone else to do it. He probably didn't think that it was important when I said it, even though I jumped up and down and waved my arms to exaggerate the point.

That word of advice to all Christians is worth repeating: *Do no attempt to begin renewal without introducing the people to the one who renews.* Each church member must be confronted with Jesus, personally answering the question, "Who do you say I am?" [Matt. 16:15]. Each person must be converted to Jesus, or he will either oppose renewal or drag his feet while it is happening.

A Definition of Renewal

One of the things I did was to develop a definition for renewal: *Renewal is a process involving teaching, inspiration, exhortation, encouragement, spiritual gifts, and ministry through which God's family grows in His life, becomes what He intends them to be, and does what He intends them to do.* The definition helped me gain an overall perspective about what we were doing as a whole body. First, I understood that we were part of a "process." As sanctification is the "process" of salvation, we as a congregation were growing in God's life daily. I saw that there are many means that God uses to bring that growth about and that God has an expectation concerning what we become and what we do.

Measuring the Success of Renewal

Everyone should want to know if he or she is on the right track, church leaders especially. During the months and years of our renewal, it became clearer that there are ways to measure how things are going. This means that church leaders can measure the success of their renewal in very specific ways—take an inventory, so to speak. The following are some of those things to observe about a congregation's life:

1. *People are being converted to Jesus Christ.* Since the foundation for all renewal is that body of converted people—those who have consciously turned their lives over to Jesus Christ— it is important that the church makes sure that *all members have personally responded to Jesus Christ.* Church leaders need to develop a system to discover if their members have indeed surrendered to Christ. For those who haven't, opportunities of teaching and exhortation must be provided. At any

given time, church leaders should be able to know the actual numbers of those who have yet to respond to Christ.

2. *Evangelism is being stressed and evidenced.* All congregations, in order to be obedient to God, must be reaching out and spreading the good news about God's kingdom. This means that the obedient congregation is always making new disciples. Evangelism, perceived only as lifestyle, falls short of obedience to God. We are all to have a Christ-like life, but we are also all called to spread the word of salvation. Leaders should be able to tell you how many were converted to Christ in the last month, in several months, or in a year. It is not a matter of keeping trophies but a matter of good Christian stewardship of the things of God. In the book of Acts, it was important that Luke tell you three thousand were saved in one day or that new converts were being added daily.

3. *The people are being converted to the church fellowship.* The local body of Christ is very important to God. It is the portion of God's family into which we are being adopted. It is crucial that each Christian recognize the significance of Christ's body and surrender her life to it. Leaders will know when people have been converted to church fellowship when they meet together regularly, share gifts, encourage each other, and do God's work together. It is in the midst of fellowship that the grave clothes are taken away, and people arise in their new lives in Christ. Leaders should know how many of their congregation demonstrate their conversion to church fellowship.

4. *People are being baptized in the Holy Spirit.* It is foundational to powerful church life that the members all have their own Pentecost experience. This empowers them to do God's work in the church and in the world. Each congregation should develop its own method for teaching and encouraging this encounter with the Holy Spirit. The leaders should be able to account for each person, knowing if this release of the Spirit has taken place.

5. *Gifts of the Spirit are being evidenced.* A congregation that is meeting in fellowship should have evidence that the Holy Spirit is active through the people. This will be apparent in the exercise of charismatic gifts. Such gifts are essential to the building up of the body of Christ. Leaders have a

responsibility to demonstrate and disciple people in the exercise of spiritual gifts. Without gifts of the Spirit, the vine withers and little fruit is produced.

6. *Fruit of the Spirit is being evidenced.* When God is at work in the lives of the people, everything changes. People are committed to being disciples, they are growing in their knowledge of Christ, they are becoming more like Him, and they are doing what He would have them do. But more than that, their character changes and each begins to exude God's life. Church leaders must be aware if such fruit is being produced, how to encourage it, and how to measure its growth.

7. *Worship and praise are overflowing.* When people are converted to Christ, converted to fellowship, and growing in God's life, then worship and praise begin to abound. This means that a person's life becomes an offering of worship, as well as the fruit of the lips. Congregations experiencing God's new life should notice changes in the worship at every meeting. When leaders meet, they will naturally want to express their love of God with their words and songs of praise and worship.

8. *The people are becoming more obedient to God.* A church in renewal will experience the dedication of its people to obey the will of God. They will listen to the Holy Spirit's nudgings, they will read and study the Word of God, and they will seek ways to be of one mind. Jesus will become Lord of the congregation, Lord of personal lives. Leaders will evidence this obedience as they meet together to discover and obey God's will for the congregation.

9. *The people are sharing their resources.* When people begin to grow in God, they also begin to tithe their resources to the body of Christ. They will give sacrificially to those in need. Church leaders demonstrate their growth in God by showing others how to give joyfully to the work of God in the church.

10. *The people are being converted to the ministry of the church.* A sign of growing in God is the desire of the people to do the ministry of the church. They will want to express God's life so that others may grow in Him; they will be willing to assume roles of leadership when asked; they will want to demonstrate good works in this hurting world. They will want to feed the poor with good food to sustain their bodies, and they

will feed them with eternal food that will sustain their souls. They will be so full of God's love that they will want to give it away to anyone who will receive it.

Parish renewal is always in process; it has no ending, and exists as long as the congregation is in existence. That is why no one ever arrives at the ultimate. That is reserved for the time when we leave this life and go on to be with Jesus permanently. When a congregation is in the process of renewal, the ministries will grow in increasing measure. What one may observe in the evidences of parish renewal is that they call for the same radical commitments of a person's life that Jesus demanded [see Matt. 5:20; 18:3; 18:35; Luke 6:20–42; 9:23–25, 60–62; 13:3–5]. Being a disciple of Jesus is not easy, for it both demands of us to leave behind old life and commands us in the new. This is not congregational life as usual. This is congregational life at its best.

If You Are Born Again You Will Know It

When Jenny was converted and began to receive what was promised at her infant baptism, it was all measurable. She knew things were different.

"As a new Christian, the part that amazes me the most is the born-again part. I really have been born again. When He says He makes all things new, He means it. I am a new creature. I can't believe this is me, yet it is what I have always hoped for. With God's grace, I have been changed. Old habits have become less desirable, and the Lord has become more desirable. I have found myself wanting more and more of Him and less of everything else.

"I owe Him my life. What I had before I wouldn't call a life. I couldn't see that then; that's why they call it walking in darkness. I wouldn't trade my life now for the world, even though it has been a struggle—I spent one and a half years with swollen eyes from crying tears I tried so hard to hide. Every step of the struggle has been worth it because of the freedom I feel now. I know He isn't finished with me; I'm sure He's only just begun."

Jenny was able to describe her awareness of being born again. If God does something in a person's life then it is describable, it is measurable. It is as measurable as John's words [1 John 1:1–3]: "That which was from the beginning, which we have heard, which we have seen with our eyes, which we have looked at and our hands have touched—this we proclaim concerning the Word of life. The life appeared; we have seen it and testify to it, and we proclaim to you the eternal life which was with the Father and has appeared to us. We proclaim to you what we have seen and heard, so that you also may have fellowship with us." Jenny and the disciples heard, saw, and touched the things of God. It was from such a personal encounter that their lives were changed; it is because of this life-changing experience that they have something to tell others. It is measurable in the sense that the person knows, and it is measurable in the sense that the community knows.

Whether we are born again or not is discernible and measurable. The question for those in leadership is whether or not they will make discipleship and the renewal of the church the worthwhile issue that it is. Returning the church back to its apostolic roots can be very painful, for there are decades of religion to undo. When a congregation returns to its apostolic roots, it aligns itself with the power that made the early church such a mighty force. Modernism, humanism, psychologism, and New Ageism have effectively removed apostolic power from many churches. Renewal restores what was lost. It teaches what the apostles taught, encourages apostolic faith, and experiences apostolic power. Renewal puts substance on the symbolism of Christianity, the same substance that grew a worldwide church.*

Being a Disciple

Church renewal has its best beginnings where there are both clergy and laity who are willing to have renewal begin with them. Each individual church is called to make disciples [see Matt. 28:19]. But to make disciples requires that we are disciples. This means that congregational leaders should be disciples before they begin discipling the people in their congregations. We are first disciples of Jesus Christ and then with those that God places in leadership over us.

The pastor is, by calling, the chief discipler of the local church. If the discipleship process works properly, the leader disciples a few leaders who in turn disciple others. After a few months, each person who is a disciple should be able to affirm these statements:

---

*Radio and TV personality Rush Limbaugh coined the definition of liberalism as "symbolism without substance." This has been the problem of the modern church. It proclaims the symbolism of Salvation, Sanctification, Justification, etc., but lacks the life-transforming properties toward which these symbols point.

1. *I have repented of my old life and renounce my claim on my future* [see Mark 1:15; Rom. 3:23; Acts 3:19; 17:30; Joel 2:13; Heb. 3:13; Luke 13:3].
2. *I have renounced the world, the flesh and the devil* [see Acts 26:17–18; John 8:42–47; 12:30–32; Heb. 2:14–18; 1 John 3:8; 2:13–17; Rom. 6:5–8].
3. *I believe the claims that Jesus made about Himself, as well as the claim the apostles made about Him* [see John 3:36; 4:14; 5:23b; 6:35–40; 7:37–39; 8:23–24; 8:58; 11:25–26; 12:44–46; 14:6; Acts 4:12; 13:39; Rom. 1:3–4; Eph. 1:7; Col. 1:15–18; 2:9; 2 Peter 1:3–4].
4. *I have surrendered my life to Jesus Christ, body, soul, mind, possessions, and future* [see Rom. 12:1; Phil. 3:12–15; Acts 4:32].
5. *I acknowledge Jesus Christ to be my Savior, and I will follow Him as my Lord* [see Acts 2:21; 16:30–31; Rom. 10:8–10; John 1:10–13].
6. *I acknowledge the Holy Spirit to be the Lord and giver of life* [see John 6:63; Rom. 8:11; 2 Cor. 3:6].
7. *I have asked Jesus to baptize me in the Holy Spirit* [see Matt. 3:11; Mark 1:8; Luke 3:16; 24:49; John 1:33; Acts 1:4–5, 8; 2:38–39; 11:15–17].
8. *I join with others in fellowship, seeking the Spirit's direction, both for my life and for the life of this congregation* [see John 15:26; 16:13; Rom. 8:14; Gal. 5:18].
9. *I believe that I must make my future with the people of God and especially with this congregation to which God has joined me. I commit myself to them fully. I offer my time, talent, and money, as well as my lack of the same* [see Acts 2:42; 4:32–35; 1 John 1:1–7].

It will be typical of many Christians to resist making strong commitments. When Jesus demanded strong commitments from his disciples [see John 6:60–69], many of them left for good.

Leaders Getting the Right Attitudes

Several years ago a group of renewal leaders came together to discuss what made renewal work in their congregations. They were asked to share what they considered to be the most important advice they could give to someone just beginning. Their responses were startling; each in his own way said that attitudes [see Phil. 2:5; Rom. 8:5–9; 12:2] about renewal were more important than any practical advice they could give. Here is a list of attitudes they thought to be all important:

1. *Be in a love relationship with the congregation—not in an adversary relationship.* God's people cannot be your enemies [see Phil. 2:1–4; John 15:12; 1 John 4:9–11].
2. *Be willing to risk an all-out commitment to the renewal of your church.* When you start something, be prepared to finish it [see Matt. 28:19].
3. *Be committed to every-member evangelism, believing that God is able to change everyone.* Otherwise you will judge yourself better than some others [see Rom. 9:16; 5:6; Acts 4:12].
4. *Be committed to follow the leadings of the Holy Spirit.* We are called to serve God's will, not the people's [see Rom. 8:14; Matt. 24:14; 1 Sam. 15:22; Eccl. 12:13].
5. *Believe that only God can cause the renewing of people and churches.* Clever ideas and programs have no transforming power [see 1 Cor. 3:6].
6. *Be committed to thinking biblically:* Scripture first, tradition next, reason last [see 2 Tim. 3:16].
7. *Be committed to proceed despite criticism.* God does not criticize and condemn; He disciplines and helps [see James 1:2–5].
8. *Understand that you cannot minister to everyone.* Jesus never ran after those who walked away from Him [see John 6:66–67; Matt. 19:21–23].
9. *Be committed to begin with those ready to begin.* God sends you those who are to begin the process; it is a mistake to wait for more [see Gal. 6:10; John 10:14,16].
10. *Be committed to pitch what you do to the highest level of maturity.* People want to be challenged, to be called higher, not to be mediocre and bland [see Col. 1:28; Matt. 5:48].
11. *Be vulnerable, not defensive.* God is capable of defending Himself and you as well; let Him [see 2 Cor. 12:9].
12. *Expect a miracle.* You will probably need a few [see Mark 10:26b-27; 9:23; 1 Cor. 4:20; 2:5].

The Return to Apostolic Life

Apostolic teaching means that we return to the authority of Scripture as being the Word of God. It means that we take seriously the words of the Bible, knowing that God speaks His truth through it. It means that Scripture offers us the guidelines for all Christian behavior, as well as a way to authenticate teaching and preaching. Apostolic teaching also means taking seriously the truth that has been given us from the earliest days of the church, truth that has endured the various tests applied. It means that the tradition (not the traditions) of the church has relevance for us today.

Apostolic faith believes and acts upon what God reveals of Himself. Whether it be the nudging of the Holy Spirit or an insight revealed in Scripture, apostolic faith puts its trust in that revelation. Apostolic faith enables Christians to be bold in the gifts and operations of the Holy Spirit and to cling to God's truth when the world speaks otherwise— when hope withers. Faith believes that God is faithfully fulfilling His Word—that everything He has promised will come true.

Renewal believes that a gospel without life-changing power is no gospel at all. This means that God, through his Holy Spirit, empowers every aspect of our Christian life. He actually gives us new life when we are born again; He fully empowers us with supernatural power with the baptism in the Holy Spirit. He fills us with His life so that we can grow in God's life, and He will come again to make everything new in the age to come.

As we understand the process of renewal, we are able to visualize the apostolic restoration taking place, and we are able to measure its effects. Good leadership focuses on the whole of it, recognizing that as changes take place, the structure of the church will change also. The way in which leaders lead and are perceived will be the first places of structural change. Leaders will not be the ones who do the ministry of the church but rather those who encourage the ministry of the entire church. They will be the disciplers, the encouragers. This will be a difficult change for many who expect the paid clergy to do ministry rather than to get others to do ministry. Every-member ministry, once accepted by the people, will lead to greater growth and excitement within the church.

Another place of structural change will be the way worship is conducted. Jesus said that we couldn't put new wine in old wineskins lest they burst. The same is true of a church in renewal. As the people are filled with new wine, they will naturally want to express themselves more freely, more openly, and in new ways. If the tradition of the church restricts this expression, then bursting is inevitable. This can fracture a congregation. For this reason, responsible leaders will make sure that the structure of worship gradually changes so that the new wine becomes no problem.

18

HOPE FOR TROUBLED CHURCHES

Mainline Denominations Have Lost Their Way

The Episcopal Church is typical of many mainline denominations today. They appear to be sold out to the world, the flesh, and the devil. This may sound judgmental, but that is exactly what Paul instructed us to do. "Are you not to judge those inside?" [1 Cor. 5:12b]. The church has allowed the world to set the agenda and the theology for the future. A lot of it began when I was in seminary. God was now dead, according to many erstwhile theologians. My seminary moved from an isolated hill in the village of Gambier, Ohio, to become more "relevant" in the city of Rochester, New York. Seminarians were now being taught that the Word of God was no longer meaningful unless it was "demythologized" for our modern culture. Clergy began to use the language of the street in churches, believing that it would make them part of "what was happening." Others encouraged free sex. Sensitivity training and encounter groups were in vogue. That was in 1962.

I didn't realize it at the time, but the Episcopal Church, along with other denominations, was beginning to lose members. It started after my ordination in 1966, and within three years it had lost nearly 112,000 members. The people knew, before the clergy, that something was wrong. It wasn't until almost five years after my ordination that I understood that the church was on the wrong track, moving contrary to God's will. The trouble was that I had become part of the clergy leadership that brought such trouble to the church. I became deeply involved in sensitivity training and began to move with the culture.

Within the next twenty-five years, the Episcopal Church in the United States lost one-third of its membership. It has not recovered yet, nor have other mainline denominations. During that same time the Roman Catholic Church was losing priests and nuns by the thousands. The once-healthy seminaries soon had but a trickle of new recruits. While the Episcopal Church was losing members, its clergy ranks were increasing. That alone should have sent up red flags. Why ordain more clergy when the clergy you have drive people out of the church? The people continued to abandon ship; they knew the course of the church could only lead to shipwreck.

It is unclear to me why church leaders failed to have a summit meeting to determine what was wrong. The people, however, did not wait; they became unchurched, or members of Baptist or Pentecostal churches. Many were hungry and thirsty for the things of God. No one can drink from a well that has gone dry. The church was no longer feeding people with God's Word, or causing them to drink of God's Spirit. The gospel no longer seemed to have the power to save and change lives, God's Word no longer had authority, and the foundations of the church had been replaced with the changing moods of relevancy.

It was not only the changing foundations of the church that caused people to leave; they were also faced with boredom. Sunday after Sunday they faced the same old liturgies, stale hymns, performance choirs, organ recitals, and boring and lifeless sermons. But worse than this, people had lost contact with the living God.

A few years ago, my wife, Jan, and I attended Sunday services at Canterbury Cathedral, the principal church of the Anglican archbishop of Canterbury. There were visitors there from all over the world who had come, as we did, to share in the wonderful heritage of our Anglican Communion, as represented by Canterbury. We had come to be inspired by the best that Anglican Christianity had to offer. Instead, the liturgy was lifeless and boring. I felt as though the clergy were unsure if God was alive and well.

The preaching was the worst part of the morning. It was a travelogue instead of a sermon. There was absolutely no gospel in the message and no mention of our Lord. I wanted to stand up and say, "That's not Christianity. That's not what it's all about. People, don't believe what you are hearing. Listen, I will tell you the good news." My wife had to restrain me as she saw my anger mount, anger over the fact that our church allowed such an inane preacher to mount that hallowed pulpit.

I have heard most all of the arguments that defend impotent ministry, such as, "God is in it even if the leader isn't," "The Holy Spirit is at work despite us," and so on. Yet I have wondered since then, "Is that the kind of church that has turned so many Episcopalians away?" And nothing has changed, it's only gotten worse in the mainline denominations. The church has gone awry, and it has not yet been fixed.

Only God Can Fix the Broken Church

I hope that it is obvious from what I have written that God has been pouring his Holy Spirit upon the churches in hopes that the leaders and people would turn to Him in surrender and utilize the power that was given to the apostolic church. The present outpouring of the Holy Spirit has come to every denomination and almost every congregation. Church leaders should not shun what God is doing, for the people are in desperate need for an authentic experience of God. They want to know if God and His kingdom are real or whether they should search for something else. They want to know if "born again" is a liturgical phrase or God's power to change their lives. They want to know if there are any absolutes on which they can depend. They want to know if there is any true hope, any meaning for life. Or do church leaders make it up as they go along?

God's outpouring has not ended; therefore, there is still hope for the mainline churches. But as He is touching us with His Holy Spirit, He is also telling us to repent and turn to Him. *Surrender* is the word. He is charging the church to renounce afresh the world, the flesh, and the devil. God wants to set the agenda for the future of the church; He doesn't want impostors doing it. He wants us to return to his Word, to trust it, knowing that it is all true. He doesn't want us to listen to the impostors who tell us that scripture no longer has authority for the life of the church.

The church that will return to the Upper Room is the church that will be filled with God's life in new and powerful ways. There will be a harvest of people who will be converted to Jesus Christ. The gifts of the Holy Spirit will abound, and we will begin to bear His fruit. People will be made whole as God demonstrates that He is the healer. Righteousness will return to the church as we reject the previous tendency to embrace the world's agenda. Jesus Christ will once again become Lord of the church, not only in word but in actuality.

Jesus Is the Builder of the Church

It is reassuring to know that God's plan for the church has not changed. As is Jesus Christ "the same yesterday and today and forever" [Heb. 13:8], so is the church. The impotent church may *appear* to be different, but the true body of Christ has the same foundations and principles as Peter preached in his first sermon on Pentecost. "Seeing what was ahead, he spoke of the resurrection of the Christ, that he was not abandoned to the grave, nor did his body see decay. God has raised this Jesus to life, and we are all witnesses of the fact. Exalted to the right hand of God, he has received from the Father the promised Holy Spirit and has poured out what you now see and hear" [Acts 2:31–33].

The foundations of the true church never change; they are never altered. Jesus is still its "chief cornerstone" [see Eph. 2:19–20], yet He becomes a stumbling block [see Isa. 8:14] for the church that fails to understand who He is. Without looking to Jesus, the "author and perfecter" [Heb. 12:2], the church will grope about as one who has lost his sight. Paul had already warned that the church must be careful how it builds itself, "For no one can lay any foundation other than the one already laid which is Christ Jesus" [1 Cor. 3:10–11] The church must be, as Harry Blamires writes, an "imitative body." Secular society has made such inroads into Christian thought that the church has opted for creativity, spontaneity, and freedom in lieu of obedience to God. In the face of attractive novelties, we may momentarily forget that the church is useful to God only in the same measure that He builds it. "Originality belongs to God," Blamires asserts. "The New Testament leaves no room for the current concept of 'creativeness.'"[1] Jesus found His creativity in the Father, the church finds creativity in Jesus.

The church would be nothing without Jesus. It is for His glory that it exists [see Eph. 3:21]. Jesus must be preached that the church may prosper. Paul said, "I planted the seed, Apollos watered it, but God made it grow. So neither he who plants nor he who waters is anything, but only God, who makes things grow" [1 Cor. 3:6–7]. It is the person of Jesus and our relationship with Him that are the foundation and substance of Christianity. Instead, we sometimes make the mistake of believing that Christianity is the *teaching* of Jesus. Such belief only assures that we will become more and more separated from a relationship with God, substituting instead principles of this world. This is why Christianity cannot be placed alongside other religions, as if they are similar. There is only one true revelation of God, and that has come to us in the person of Jesus Christ [see Heb. 1:1–3]. Without Jesus we become a religious club. When Jesus is at the heart of the church, as He should be, then He becomes its builder; if He is the builder, then nothing is impossible for it [see Luke 1:37]. The same supernaturally creative process that brought the Earth into existence is at work in an obedient church. For this reason, the church today can be at least as powerful as was the church described in the book of Acts. Whatever was possible for Peter, Paul, and Luke is still possible for us. Jesus does not change, nor does his true church.

NOTES

LEARNING TO LEAD PEOPLE TO JESUS

[1]*The Book of Common Prayer* (New York: Church Hymnal Corporation, 1979), 857.
[2]C. B. Moss, *The Christian Faith* (New York: S.P.C.K., 1954), 343.
[3]Ibid., 341.
[4]Ibid., 247.
[5]David Watson, *I Believe in the Church* (Grand Rapids, Mich.: Eerdmans, 1978), 309.
[6]William A. Leonard, *The Witness of the American Church to Pure Christianity* (New York: James Pott, 1894), 9.
[7]Leon Joseph Cardinal Suenens, *A New Pentecost?* (Glasgow: Collins, Fountain Books, 1978), 168.
[8]Harry Blamires, *Where Do We Stand?* (Ann Arbor, Mich.: Servant Books, 1980), 41.
[9]Suenens, *A New Pentecost?*, 171.

CONFRONTING THE DEMONIC

[1]Cyril of Jerusalem, *The Library of Christian Classics*, vol. 4 (Philadelphia: Westminster Press, 1955), 70–71.

LEARNING TO BE A HEALING CHURCH

[1]George Eldon Ladd, *The Gospel of the Kingdom* (Grand Rapids, Mich.: Eerdmans, 1983), 22–23.
[2]Augustine, *The Library of Christian Classics*, vol. 8, 263–264.
[3]Moss, *The Christian Faith*, 169.

[4]John Wimber, *Healing: Categories and Operatives,* vol. 3 (Placentia, Calif.: Vineyard Christian Fellowship), 7.

[5]Suenens, *A New Pentecost?,* 156.

[6]Irenaeus, *Library of Christian Classics,* vol. 1, 377.

BACK TO THE UPPER ROOM

[1]Charles E. Hummel, *Fire in the Fireplace* (Downers Grove, Ill.: InterVarsity, 1978), 94–95.

[2]R. A. Torrey, *The Person and Work of the Holy Spirit* (Grand Rapids, Mich.: Zondervan Publishing House, 1974), 170.

[3]Ibid., 173.

LEARNING TO PRAISE AND WORSHIP

[1]*Charles Finney, an Autobiography* (Old Tappan, N.J.: Revell, 1908), 20.

[2]Moss, *The Christian Faith,* 246–248.

[3]*The Book of Common Prayer,* 42.

DISCOVERING WHERE GOD IS LEADING

[1]*The Book of Common Prayer,* 854.

[2]Blamires, *Where Do We Stand?,* 94–95.

[3]Everett L. Fullam, *Facets of the Faith* (Lincoln, Va.: Chosen Books, 1982), 34.

[4]J. N. D. Kelly, *Early Christian Doctrines* (San Francisco: Harper and Row, 1978), 190–191.

LEARNING TO RAISE UP LAY MINISTRY

[1]Michael Harper, *Let My People Grow* (Plainfield, N.J.: Logos International, 1977), 88.

[2]David Watson, *Called and Committed* (Wheaton, Ill.: Harold Shaw, 1982), 74.

LEARNING TO LIVE IN FELLOWSHIP

[1]Seunens, *A New Pentecost?,* 141.

[2]Augustine, *The Library of Christian Classics,* vol. 8, 163.
[3]*The Book of Common Prayer,* 336.

LEARNING HOW TO CHOOSE LEADERS

[1]Charles Wesley, "And Can It Be?" (Eastbourne, U.K.: Kingsway, 1987), 12.
[2]Harper, *Let My People Grow,* 219.
[3]Ibid., 218.
[4]Hans Kung, *On Being a Christian* (Garden City, N.Y.: Doubleday, 1976), 484–487.
[5]*Dictionary of Pentecostal and Charismatic Movements,* (Grand Rapids, MI: Regency Reference Library, Zondervan Publishing House, 1988), 247.

HOPE FOR TROUBLED CHURCHES

[1]Blamires, *Where Do We Stand?,* 60–61.